Legends and
Prophecies of the
QUERO APACHE

"Maria is blessed by the Giver of All Life, and protected by the Ancient Ones. She is not of one clan, one people— she belongs to humanity and has endured much that has tempered her spirit and opened her mind's eye. Knowledge is within her. She continues to discover it."

Ten Bears, Apache Tlish Diyan Godiyihgo

Legends and Prophecies of the
QUERO APACHE

Tales for Healing and Renewal

Maria Yracébûrû

Bear & Company
Rochester, Vermont

Bear & Company
One Park Street
Rochester, Vermont 05767
www.InnerTraditions.com

LIBRARY OF CONGRESS CATALOGING-IN-PUBLICATION DATA
Yracébûrû, Maria.
Legends and prophecies of the Quero Apache / Maria Yracébûrû.
p. cm.
ISBN 1-879181-77-0
1. Apache mythology. 2. Apache Indians—Folklore.
3. Tales—Arizona. I. Title.
E99.A6 Y73 2002
398.2'089'972—dc21
2002000688

Printed and bound in the United States

10   9   8   7   6   5   4   3   2   1

Interior illustrations by Maria and Lynda Yracébûrû
Text design by Virginia Scott Bowman
This book was typeset in Granjon with Papyrus as the display typeface

For Jeremy and Jason,
Mariana, Cheri, and Lynda,
And especially for the continuance. . . .
For my granddaughters,
Marianna and Gabriella,
with love.

twilight dancing in Snake's eyes
dewy pearls in the recesses of my mind
diamond icicles stretched across time
call to me across a fine line
calling and whispering,
"you are mine. . . ."

Contents

The Family Tree

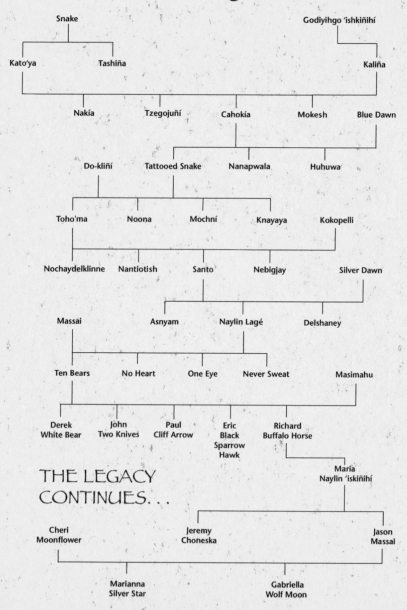

Snake — Godiyihgo 'ishkiñihí

Kato'ya — Tashiña   Kaliña

Nakía   Tzegojuñí   Cahokia   Mokesh   Blue Dawn

Do-kliñí   Tattooed Snake   Nanapwala   Huhuwa

Toho'ma   Noona   Mochní   Knayaya   Kokopelli

Nochaydelklinne   Nantiotish   Santo   Nebigjay   Silver Dawn

Massai   Asnyam   Naylin Lagé   Delshaney

Ten Bears   No Heart   One Eye   Never Sweat   Masimahu

Derek White Bear   John Two Knives   Paul Cliff Arrow   Eric Black Sparrow Hawk   Richard Buffalo Horse

Maria Naylin 'iskiñihí

THE LEGACY CONTINUES...

Cheri Moonflower   Jeremy Choneska   Jason Massai

Marianna Silver Star   Gabriella Wolf Moon

Acknowledgments

This book owes so much to so many that I cannot thank them all. Behind my knowledge are the true authors of this book: all the Spirits, including those of my ancestors, whose lives were my models and whose courage and determination enabled them to pass the legends and prophecies on to me. Various students and relatives have served as audiences for honing my storytelling skills: my sons, Jeremy and Jason Tucker, my uncle Woody Sa'ch Bailey, my auntie Kalei Woodsong Muller, Yvonne White Corn Farley, Deni Breath of Life and Roger Gray Otter Halterman, Fran Blue Swallow Hughey, Linda Clear Water Scott, and Jay Rocksong Ruiz. I am honored to have their love and presence in my life. To the late JoAnn Lo-n-timi Miles, who was, and is, a constant source of inspiration, I say: *Ukehe, Lo-n-timi.*

Arielle Ford, who first asked me to participate in one of her *Hot Chocolate Mysticism* anthologies, has helped make it possible for me to turn my ideas into a book. Without her help and encouragement I would never have gotten it done.

Stephanie Gunning's editing helped me add both the information and healing qualities that had slipped past my limited perception.

My *houshté* (life partner), Lynda, has encouraged and inspired me for years, and has tolerated paper trash on the floor of the living room as well as the time I was lost in my work for too long. Honey, we did it!

Introduction:
Threshold to Tomorrow

In August 1881 a short stocky man, gently cradling a goose-wing fan and a pollen bag, stood before a hundred Apache during a secret religious ceremony and dared to challenge the most elusive renegades to hold a world vision that would not even begin to manifest until a century later. Among those gathered to hear the prophet, the Coyotero Apache medicine man Nochaydelklinne, were his niece, Naylin Lagé, and her young son, Ten Bears.

Ten Bears was born in Old Mexico, shortly before the end of the Apache Wars. No one is quite certain of the exact date. The stories he told of his childhood and youth, on the run with his renegade parents, would place him between 103 and 105 years of age when he left this plane of existence in 1973. During his youth, Ten Bears was instructed by his mother, a *Tlish Diyan* healer and apprentice to the prophet. This training laid the foundation for Ten Bears' beliefs in the philosophy, legends, and visions that had been handed down for generations.

As a child he was taught to gather the many riches of the earth from the land for his mother, who prepared and used them to help others who crossed their life path. By the time he was twenty he had charted the stars for the ceremonial cyclic year and had run each and every one of the eleven rites that honor and bless the evolutionary process of Earth Mother and humanity.

In his later years he worked closely with other Native American Elders who carried the oral traditions, legends, and prophecies in secrecy. These were not secretive until fairly recent historic times, and there were two primary reasons for the development of that secrecy.

First, the ancestors of modern-day Native Americans discovered that non-Natives did not take their religions seriously. They were ridiculed and labeled superstitions. This tendency was established as early as the first visit of Christopher Columbus, who wrote in his journal about the people he mistakenly called Indios, "They appear to have no religion." New England Puritans would later call Native religious practices "devil worship." And as recently as the mid-1990s the Pope stated there was no evidence of Native sacred sites or religion. Faced with these kinds of attitudes about deeply held beliefs, Native Americans began to keep information about their religions to themselves. Why tell anyone? Why be subjected to ridicule or insult?

The second, and perhaps the most significant, historical reason for the development of this secrecy was safety. In the United States, laws were long in effect forbidding the practice of Native religions. As late as 1911, Creek Indians were attacked and killed by members of the Oklahoma National Guard for participating in a religious ceremony. Today, even with the American Indian Religious Freedom Act, the Native American Church is regarded as an illegal gathering in many states.

However, Ten Bears and many other Elders knew from the

prophecies handed down by the Ancient Ones that the time would come to share. Ten Bears clearly saw the disastrous results of silence, then commonly sanctioned by all societies of the world. He taught the philosophy and understanding of the Sacred Universal Laws; the hippie movement of the 1960s was his first sign that the time—the shift in consciousness—had occurred.

My first memories of Ten Bears were of his winsome smile, his cheeriness, and his playfulness. His nickname for me was Little One, doubtless because of my size; even now, as a grandmother, I only stand five feet even. I'm not exactly sure when I began to follow him around, learning the value of a life steeped in tradition. I'd like to believe that who I am today has a lot to do with the encouragement to accentuate the positive, which he supplied throughout my formative years.

I am Ten Bears' granddaughter, the hereditary recipient of his philosophy, legends, prophecy, knowledge, and tradition. He sang to me the songs of great leaders who believed in peace. He sat with me many days, teaching me the way of the Tlish Diyan, the Snake Clan, teaching me the ways of humans and spirits alike, telling me the legends and prophecies of evolution.

The world that I grew up in was inhabited by people whose life philosophy is now contained deep within the well of my being, and it gives my life both coherence and direction. The land of my experience and the legends is found in a small canyon near McNary, Arizona, which links me to the spirits of the Apache Tlish Diyan and the elemental energies of the land. I understood from the legends and prophecies that I was living in a shared environment that was both sacred and mysterious. My world is one that expresses a profound spiritual awareness of the Divine Power of which all natural phenomena are manifestations.

The call to share the prophecies and legends at this time is part of my family's work; you could say I promote healing. As a mixed blood I am the fulfillment of the Rainbow Prophecy; from my mother's belly and my father's loins, a half-breed of purpose. I am a seal between cultures. One of many.

When I was seventeen I was called to return to my ancestral homeland. Ten Bears had announced his intent to cross over to the Place of Souls. I remember how his face lit up and his eyes shone as he spoke of the legends and prophecies I was now to share with the world, legends and prophecies that would "greatly release human suffering." After making this statement he rose from his favorite spot on the porch of our canyon home, kissed us all goodnight, and went peacefully to sleep, by choice, to be laid to rest in the heart of his beloved Earth Mother.

But the evolution continues. And as thousands continue to seek Ten Bears' wisdom, the original tradition of the Quero Tlish Diyan, the legends live on, even stronger than in his lifetime.

I learned from Ten Bears, and he learned from his mother, Naylin Lagé, who learned from Nochaydelklinne. The legends speak about life. They are a living reflection of the past aiding the present, a way of seeing the timeless and universal link between humans, Creation, and nature. They are important for everyone, since all people and beings sharing this planet can benefit from their wisdom. They are a way in which strength and knowledge can be experienced today, passing healthy, functional relationships from generation to generation.

Wholeness is discovered with time. Self-empowerment is medicine, and healing is strength—strength to rediscover and re-create the spiritual connection and compassion in the present. The legends and prophecies in this book are therefore a map; they guide us home. And they have been with me for as long as I can remember.

The legends of the Tlish Diyan relay how, when human beings

were first created, we were given a nature-based life philosophy to guide our steps of evolution. The Sacred Universal Laws govern our relationship to the natural world, our interaction with nature, and our respect for each other. These laws celebrate humanity's relationship with nature and other humans, and they may easily be seen daily simply by looking without and within. These legends are a source of guidance, teaching, and, in some cases, entertainment to help us in our daily lives.

Although the legends are very old they should not be considered relics of the past. The value of their lessons cannot be ignored, and the messages of love for all and respect for self must be embraced—this is our evolutionary task. Now more than ever the legends and prophecies of the Tlish Diyan—with their lessons of love, mutual respect, and awareness of responsibility—must be embraced, actualized, and passed on. They are the strength of a whole, healed, spiritual Fifth World of Peace and Illumination.

The time is now for all to benefit and heal with Changing Mother. We must share Earth, listen to the legends, heal, and live in peace with each other, and in harmony with All Our Relations. It is here and now that the legends and prophecies speak, exemplifying the benefits of healing dysfunction and the clarification that comes with self-actualization. They speak of evolving community, lessons, celebrations, rites of passage, and healing that help maintain and regain wholeness through remembering the important principles of responsible co-creation.

I am sure Ten Bears would challenge you to participate in this adventure of self-discovery and recognition of the Universal Family. Human evolution is our beloved lifelong project, and it is now our charge to create conditions that are favorable to the healing of humanity's soul and will ease the process of transition into the Fifth World of Peace and Illumination.

These legends and prophecies continue to supply the interest and doorways of opportunity that open in a synchronistic manner as we travel the path the Ancestors charted centuries ago. Grandpa was a forward-looking man and eager to share the valuable information of our tradition and the basic laws of nature with everyone. Inspired by years of traditional living and Ten Bears' example, I live for this day. I continually strive to make available a large amount of practical knowledge for healing that helps to achieve and maintain the balanced, harmonious lifestyle that embraces the beauty of life.

Your participation in the birthing of a new world, therefore, is greatly honored by the Old Ones. Undoubtedly, a heartstring will be plucked as you are enfolded within the energy of remembrance. If you are confronted by the illusion of fear think of the images presented in these legends and prophecies. Gather your inner vision and see the visions on the backs of your eyelids. The images will provide a sense of knowing and connection that can get you through confusing times.

Feel a surge of experienced love and protection. Years that at one point seemed to fly slowly with deep deliberation, like blue herons, now speed by, like the flickering wing-darts of a swooping swallow. The world is changing quickly. With the end of the Fourth World of Separation, humanity must look out across the land-sense and feel the tranquillity, the calmness that is so very powerful. That is what keeps humanity alive, being One with this all-encompassing power. This power comes from the natural environment—from a mesa, a rock, a beach, a mountain. There's something that emanates from the land we call Mother that is all-healing. Once we get in touch with that force, once we become centered and can realize and attempt to understand it and make it part of us, we can pretty much co-create anything because we know that whatever is out there is also inside of us.

The thirteen stories in this book are prayers and celebrations. They are given in joy for Earth Mother and for our healing, because we need healing right now. They reflect a past steeped in tradition and reverence and the promise of a future of hope and peace. It is time to embrace the ethics of the Fifth World: love, a heart of compassion, the virtue of health, humility of ego, forbearance with one another, forgiveness of one another, and freedom from the Shadow of Fear.

While this vision has come to me through the traditions of the Tlish Diyan, the wisdom it contains belongs to no nationality, no religion. It is far beyond the conceptions of even the most brilliant human being, so it cannot be the property of one race or culture. The need to understand the prophecies of the indigenous peoples of the world is universal; we just give those insights different names, different symbolism, in our native languages. The wisdom of the legends I present is that of the very essence of life itself, so that those who are alive will always have the possibility of knowing their connection to All That Is. This divine connection is meant to be found in the here and now, and it is within the grasp of any sincere seeker.

To you, in search of peace and unity, the sanctuary of the legends calls. My sincere hope is that these stories will nudge you to make a leap of faith, and that Spirit will make apparent to you how you may help manifest your vision of the new paradigm.

My uncles, my forefathers, have said, "This is the way it's done. Keep it up. Teach others that come, so that they will carry this forward. When you have that connection in your heart it will always carry forward."

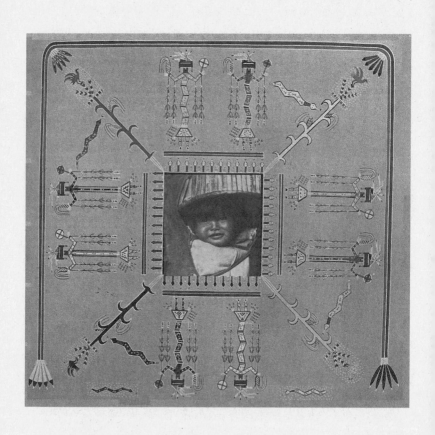

Creation

As I have previously stated, I am Quero Apache Tlish Diyan. I am a Child of the Universe. I am a half-breed, with origins in the White Mountains of Arizona. My true name is Naylin 'iskiñihí. Naylin Lagé was my great-grandmother's name. I am a storyteller in the traditional way of my ancestors. I share stories that have been handed down from one generation to another. That is my purpose. If I do not share, how can there be continuance?

Stories are sacred. They contain many layers of truth. Stories bring to life wisdom, humor, history, and prophecy. I would like to share a story with you today. Hold it or share it with love and respect when you move on in your life. Gather wisdom and embrace it as your own. When I began writing Legends and Prophecies of the Quero Apache I approached the East in a humbling way and prayed for guidance and clarity. Since East is the *direction of Spirit, I was soon enveloped in love and my creativity flowed forth. During the writing of "Creation" I was reminded that without movement nothing could be created in this universe. The revolution of the Generational Wheel was inviting me to contribute this work with the hope of generating an alternative perception on evolution and the history of Turtle Island. The scope and diversity of the story provided me with initiative and presented a spontaneous movement in tandem with the creative flow, a movement that generated a world of harmonious interaction.*

The Legend

In a remote time when there was nothing except the eternal power of All That Is, that power thought outward into space. It thought and breathed and sang, and it gave existence to two energies. So stories, like webs spun in the Mind of All, began with All That Is.

From the energy concentrated by All That Is, the Giver of All Life formed himself, announcing upon completion, "I am I." In a similar manner Changing Mother, Earth, became manifest.

The Giver of All Life lay next to his beloved Changing Mother in the Sacred Lodge and said, "Behold here how wonderful is the work of All That Is, created in our being." And he gazed upon his bride. There in that most sacred of lodges Changing Mother and the Giver of All Life, symbolizing female and male, thought and language, came together to love the universe into being. Every dimension of life was organized and given prayer.

On the first day Changing Mother and the Giver of All Life gave birth to their daughter, Spider. Spider was a very good weaver. With beautiful energy she wove paths for her siblings, and more joined her each instant. And so it was that Sun, Moon, Stars, Wind, and Rainbow were also born on that first day of life.

On the second day Changing Mother and the Giver of All Life gave birth to all the things that crawl and fly, like birds, reptiles, worms, and insects.

On the third day they gave life to the four-legged creatures of the world: the buffalo, deer, elk, antelope—all the ones that walk with hair on them.

On the fourth day they gave life to the two-legged creatures, the humans. The first two-leggeds were born in the Land of Eternal Winter in a house of ice and crystal on the shores of the big lake called Water That You Cannot See Over. On the shores of that lake Changing Mother bore twin sons. She brought them into this world as she had birthed everything preceding.

The first boy's name was Killer of Enemies. The second son's name was Child of Water. It was very cold in the home of Winter, and Changing Mother needed a way to keep the twins warm. In order for her to do this, she dug a hole in the embankment, put her sons in the hole, placed a flat rock on top, and lit a fire. The rock slowly heated and then retained the heat for a long time, warming the children as Changing Mother nursed them and raised them to become men.

Their father, the Giver of All Life, gave the two young men presents. In one hand he held an arrow from which glowed a shimmering blue light. The first born, Killer of Enemies, took the arrow. In his other hand the Giver of All Life held the datura, a medicine plant, which glowed the colors of its iridescent foliage. Child of Water took the plant.

The two brothers were Spirit Warriors, so when they were young the Giver of All Life called all of Creation together. He said,

"Because life is part of an infinite pattern, a continuum of cycles within cycles, you will be called on to instruct your younger siblings. The spinning of your mother reflects the cycles of the seasons, and the circular journey of individual manifested life mirrors this larger pattern. It is a journey you all share."

He told Sun, "They will greet you in the morning light, and you will shine down and bathe them in my unconditional love. You will honor their songs as they greet you."

He told Moon, "They will look to you for answers contained within their own hearts. Through you they will learn that their lives are sacred multidimensional circles orbited by the rise and fall of your loving vibration."

He told Stars, "Through your maps these two-leggeds will learn to keep records and see cycles locked together like the fingers of their hands. You shall teach them how to observe and keep the mind, heart, and feelings in balance."

To Wind he said, "The very sacredness of life is the celebration of change, and change will keep them grounded to Changing Mother. Wind is the magical messenger that carries with it all of this knowledge."

And finally to Rainbow he said, "They must have harmony to keep moving in constant fluctuation with the nurturing energy of Changing Mother. You are the symbol of hope, undying love, and balance. Through you, they will root their faith in the future."

Then the Giver of All Life called to Eagle and said, "Call to your younger brothers, guide them always. Speak through their times of blindness, call them. They will pay attention. Call them from the corners of their sleeping minds. Teach them to be living examples of Spirit's Call." At this time the Giver of All Life gave Eagle two names: Itzá, the White Tail; and Esau, the Yellow Tail.

Then the Giver of All Life called on Buffalo and said, "You will teach them how the circle is without end. There is no time element on any part of it. The sacredness of anything is what they allow it to be. The circle will remind them and bring them closer together, together in harmony—the harmony of blending, forgiving, loving, and tolerating. When they kill you for sustenance there will be an understanding and honoring of your sacrifice so that they might live; and they will possess the knowledge that in time the circle will turn and they will give up their bodies, from which things will grow that your family might have food. Sustaining life—a circle, one of many great circles of the sacred spiral—is your lesson to the two-leggeds." And the Buffalo accepted with good grace his purpose in the world.

The Giver of All Life then called Bear. To her he said, "To you they will offer the sunset prayer and their gratitude for a day well lived before their minds drift into Dreamtime. Within Dreamtime you will teach them how pure intent may manifest into powerful co-creative acts. You will help them to strengthen universal family ties, to renew personal commitment to growth, and to participate in projecting their dreams of peace and harmony."

Next was Owl, to whom the Giver of All Life said, "You will escort them as they leave this plane of existence. With honor they will be received in the Place of Souls. They will return to light, to beauty, and to joy when the purpose of this life is done, and they will continue on into the next life—growing ever stronger, wiser, and richer in the knowledge of self." Owl, being quite honored by this divine mission, bowed reverently.

And so it went on through the sixty-four clans, until at last only two remained: Snake and Coyote. "Snake," the Giver of All Life began, "you will teach them to actualize Spirit so that they may embrace the world and their time here with joy. You will help them to train their senses so that they may honor all things. You will teach them to savor earthly pleasures with spiritual joy. You will teach them to transmute negativity. With your approach their senses will awaken and the doors of their hearts will open. You will teach them respect for who they are."

When Coyote stepped forward to receive his assignment the silence was deafening. Coyote had already acquired a reputation for joy, frivolity, and humor; and the Giver of All Life, in his infinite wisdom, understood the importance of laughter in healing. And so he instructed Coyote, "You shall be a mirror for the two-leggeds. In your foolishness they will learn the responsibility of conscious co-creation. You will carry the balance of sacredness and irreverence required to hold open the doorway between dimensions. Through your teachings they will stay in touch with the Source of All Creation. Every act will be a spiritual act, every day a spiritual day. Thus the two-leggeds will live a spiritual life, co-creating their existence as they go."

In the Beginning . . .

Become still and aware of your breathing. Breathe to the rhythm of nature. Breathe with the Winds of Change, the four seasons. Breathe with the four elements. Breathe in the scent of herbs and the smoke of burning wood. Send out your breath to the Four Directions, to the Winds of Change . . . to North . . . to South . . . to East . . . to West. You are the Fifth Direction, at the center of your circle. Also be aware of two more directions: Above and Below.

Remember walking across the young green grass as a child. There was a special quality of light that surrounded you. Pure light seemed to come from everywhere. Everything was immersed in light. Colors were exquisitely clear and vivid. A fragile golden butterfly touched a flower and it seemed to be touching you too. You could hear the hum of bees in the sweet-scented wildflowers. A bird trilled a bright melody. Maybe a soft breeze lightly stroked your hair, curved around your body, caressed your skin and then disappeared.

Your heart beat in tempo with your breathing; you heard and felt it. Perchance something swells in your breast even now as you dwell on memories of connection, something proud and grateful and heartwarming.

As you read the stories contained within this collection allow the pinyon pine and ancient cedar trees to whisper to you. Feel the cool refreshing shadows. Hear the stream move slowly, tinkling over rocks and through the trees. Deep dark green plants whisper, whisper in the breeze. Within these stories there are the sounds of birds, of the wind. Allow your imagination to take you to another time and place. Feel like a child again.

As children growing up we were told stories. Words are sacred to a child. We have grandmothers and grandfathers who instructed us, who taught us, who gave us words. They are the Elders of our communities, our villages, our homes. We grew up with Elders always around us. One day it will be our turn. And we will have others coming to us. Hungry for words, hungry for stories. But what do we tell them? What do we say to them?

Maybe we tell how the first word came into being. That listening is the very first step toward making that discovery. That everything is connected to a moment, to a life-giving force set in motion by the first breath of so long ago.

This is a timeless reality in a vast, vast perception. It is a world that prophecies and legends foretold. We are its people. Nurtured in the womb of Changing Mother, steeped in the unconditional love, pulses the long awaited Fifth World of Peace and Illumination.

In my culture, the highest form of knowledge is revealed knowledge. To the traditional Apache the world is a world in which all things are interrelated. To us spiritualism is a part of everyday life.

Who are we? We have traveled many lifetimes, possessing extraordinary passion and dedication. Though we have walked Changing Mother many times, only a few lifetimes are remembered. For many centuries the cycles of the Fourth World of Separation turned slowly, leaving hearts clouded in smoke and ashes. Now it is our task to remember, to reconnect to the Source of All Creation. In this way the bond between humanity and Spirit is strengthened.

2
Killer of Enemies
Battles Snake

From the South, whose energy deals with the emotions and trust—the trust of a child, the love of humanity—I faced the crystalline desert light of my ancestral homeland and learned how to utilize my dreams. In Dreamtime I could fly, dip, turn, and flutter like a bird at will. It was fun capturing the patterns of the wind on feathers of hope. I discovered that when I moved in harmony with the forces of nature I was part of something powerful. Utilizing this knowledge I put pen to paper to transcribe "Killer of Enemies Battles Snake." In the process I received nurturing from the natural forces. I reaffirmed my acceptance of the way they work and expressed gratitude for my connection to that power. When initiative and natural forces are combined, there is true harmony.

The Legend

Before the Giver of All Life turned his path skyward and became invisible, he explained that the people must migrate south to find their permanent home. This is the way it was. The twin sons of Changing Mother and the Giver of All Life led the people, knowing there would be tests along the way. They scouted ahead to where they wanted to go. They persisted, keeping the doors at the top of their heads open.* They knew the purpose and the meaning of the migration.

The migration was a purification ceremony and an activation of the magnetic polar axis of Earth, Changing Mother. The people were not afraid of the polar extremities at this time; they learned that the power given them by the Giver of All Life would sustain them. So these people finally came to a place where there was steam coming out of the ground. They settled there.

Snake had previously made this place his home, and he had begun the arduous adventure of raising two children, twins Tashiña and Kato'ya. The racket of the new neighbors getting settled greatly disturbed the slumber of these two little ones, until Snake finally tired of the situation and descended swiftly to the two-legged village.

Snake blinked at the first man he saw, then finally hissed, "Stop the noise; my children need sleep. If you cannot respect others, please go elsewhere." Snake opened his mouth wide and exposed his large fangs. At this the man's courage broke and he turned and ran away as fast as he could.

During Council that evening the man falsely told the people,

---

*The phrase "the doors at the top of their heads" refers to the Quero Apache term *kopave*, which corresponds to the energy center located at the top of the cranium, commonly known as the crown chakra.

"Nothing can be done. If we stay, Snake will kill us all."

The people were in despair. "What shall we do?" they cried. Now, Killer of Enemies had taken an oath to protect the people. He said, "I must set things right. I will have to fight my uncle, the Snake."

Then Killer of Enemies girthed himself for war. He colored his body with paint as red as blood so that he might be filled with the power of Changing Mother. He made himself twelve feet tall. He used two clamshells as earrings for the power of growth. In his hair he put a hundred black eagle feathers to help him find solutions and a hundred white eagle feathers to help him heal miraculously if injured. He painted yellow rings around his eyes to bring clarity to his vision. Then he twisted his mouth into a snarl and made himself look ferocious. There had never been war before and he imagined that this was how a great warrior might look.

He stamped the earth and made his mother tremble for the first time in known history. He uttered a fierce war cry, and it echoed and re-echoed from all the mountains. He grasped his arrow, which was sharp as a weasel's tooth. "Now I am going," he said, striding forth among thunder and lightening, with mighty eagles circling above him. Thus Killer of Enemies came to the Doorway of the Snake.

"Uncle," he yelled. "I come to fight you—kill you, if need be!" They fought. The mountains shook. The earth split open. Mighty trees were splintered.

Snake opened his huge mouth and bit Killer of Enemies on the ankle. Killer of Enemies hovered near death for four days, and with the dawn of the fourth day came a powerful vision.

The Vision

Killer of Enemies saw rainbow-colored, gorgeous garlands of human devotion encircling Changing Mother's feet with ever present love.

Killer of Enemies beheld the Sacred Dance of the Giver of All Life in the twinkling stars. He saw the Sacred Dance of Light in the blue-bells and starlings. The Giver of All Life's footsteps echoed over bounding billows of Northern Lights. Killer of Enemies beheld the fantastic Dance of Life in the Canyons of Evolution. But the calm grace of Changing Mother's blissful face remained hidden behind clouds of barely perceptible truths and illusory veils created by Killer of Enemies' fearful thoughts.

Killer of Enemies waited long to see his mother's face. His patience was burned by the flame of his desire to be One and to be embraced by his mother. In the confusion of searching for his mother, he burned the sky. He ignited the stars. He melted the binding Web of Life. The heavenly fires and lights lost their balance in space and plunged headlong into the infinite darkness. Space became shadowed, Killer of Enemies' mind clouded, and all shifted before the strong burst of his fear.

His powerful energy consumed everything. As the shimmering arms of his love sought frantically to embrace and hold Changing Mother the heart of his loving light was broken; the void within his soul laughed at him from everywhere.

Killer of Enemies' light wept dewdrops of twinkling stars, until all space was filled with the fragments of his light. The crying flame of his soul called aloud for Changing Mother. In the echo of eternal space, Killer of Enemies heard his mother's response, which said without sound: "I, Changing Mother, am the light of your love—which has swallowed up everything in one light! You have searched for me outside of yourself and, by doing so, have kept me far at bay. Seek me no more apart from yourself. Seek me no more beyond the boundaries of your heart. I am you and you are me!"

On the fifth day, Killer of Enemies awoke. And as his eyes opened his uncle, Snake, who had stayed by his side throughout his time of torment, spoke: "What is past is past; it is the present and the future that concern us. Listen well, for these are my last words for you. My time here is drawing to an end. A new cycle begins.

"Remember we are all family, we must nurture each other. All must act as One. You must have one fire.

"Killer of Enemies, you are a mighty warrior. Your strength is like that of a giant pine tree whose roots spread far and deep so that it can withstand any storm. Be the protector of the two-leggeds. Protect them from their own Shadow of Fear.

"You are cunning. You are skilled. From the northern axis you shall be guardian of your sacred mother.

"Let my words sink deep into your heart and mind. Retire now to take counsel among your own. Tell them my family will teach them how to act responsibly."

Healing Shattered Reality

The illusions that pull us into fear are numerous and appear deceptively real. Some are formed in the present, but most are rooted in childhood and earlier. Killer of Enemies has shown us where this shadow that shackles so many of us took form.

It is in our identities as humans that our responsibilities lie. We cannot allow ourselves to be hobbled by woes and alienation, by feelings of inadequacy imposed on us by others. It is our responsibility to overcome these fears, to succeed in our own hearts.

This story and its characters are nothing more than the holiest aspects of your own mind; they are not other beings from some distant time. Your own inner spirit will grant gifts of knowledge and power. Accept what comes your way without doubt and without fear. You can trust your connection. The Sacred Parents will never desert you, because you can never desert yourself. This trust dissolves fear and regret. You will find a resolution to your inner conflicts. Spirit will direct you forward to the very border of reality itself. On the other side is vast profundity, the ultimate nature of existence. But the border can be crossed only if you have resolved your fear and regret.

All fear comes from our sense of self. When we stand at the border of reality we are afraid that we will lose our identities by plunging in. We are afraid of being destroyed. But we came from All That Is and the Sacred Parents in the first place. We are All That Is. To return to All That Is is to become one with Entirety. In that realization, there is no need for fear.

Whenever you begin to feel fear you may call upon your medicine power—the innate ability we each carry to connect to and communicate with all other forms of energy in a partnership of co-creation. Once you take a few cleansing breaths you will feel stronger and the discomfort will no longer bother you.

Try it.

Imagine warmth radiating through you now. Feel the relief. Your medicine power grows with your remembrance. Summon your medicine now. Allow the truth of Killer of Enemies' story to live in your heart. In your meditations remember and smile.

Early in my life I created problems for myself because I thought I needed to be more than what I was. I was afraid that I was inadequate for the destiny that had been placed before me, afraid that my being a half-breed somehow made me less equipped to carry on the stories, afraid my own people would resent me. At times the fear would be so strong that it hindered me; it prevented full involvement in the experiences I was given. I withdrew from situations in order to save myself from failure; I chose instead another kind of failure—failure to take in all I could from life, failure to be all that I could be. Every experience is designed to move us forward in the understanding of ourselves. When we withdraw we stay stuck in a world we need to leave behind.

Igniting the Storyteller's Fire

Whenever I feel the stirring within I take comfort in the knowledge that I am part of something that is greater than any clan, religion, or race. Indeed, feeling the wind, hearing the mountains sing, and having Grandfather Sun on my face create in me an all-encompassing power that can never be taken away. There are places in the world that speak of magic, places that touch and fill the heart until it aches with longing for all that is rare and wondrous and intangible to all but the Spirit. Apachería is such a place.

I used to sit for hours admiring the range of dazzling colors: reds, oranges, and yellows where the bare bones of the desert mountains lay exposed to the rays of Grandfather Sun; purples in the shadows; greens on high forested hills; and eye-burning white with uncountable variations of gray where gathering thunderclouds had lowered to rest upon the flat-topped summits.

As I sat and pondered the many ways I might relate to you how this illusion—this fear—first began to plague the two-leggeds of this world, I heard singing. It was soft. The energy distorted the air, making everything appear wavy and unclear. The singing grew louder, yet sounded like an echo. Dizziness momentarily engulfed me.

I closed my eyes and saw the cinders of a fire, flickering red lights like fireflies suddenly brought to life by the stirring of a stick. "Move back, Little One." I looked to my right and saw Grandfather. I looked at him with respect and adoration, as a vision unfolded before me.

"Come sit with me," said his lady friend, Squash Rock, patting the ground between her and my grandfather. Squash Rock's dimming black eyes reflected the flames of the fire, and it was clear she held the lessons of age. She flashed her wise eyes at me.

Sighing, I looked at Grandfather's gratified, knowing smile. "This is good, what you do," he said with a big hug. My grandfather was a man whose eyes always glistened with some secret merriment. They held a dignity but also saw the humor in life, for his life had a lot of irony in it.

Over the years of my youth we laughed together, cried together, and shared secrets. He taught me to stand in the moonlight and pay homage to my namesake, to feel a gladness that I had been born, to hear the cry of the eagle, the high-pitched call of the coyote—the connection to the land that could remove all fear of alienation.

I said a little prayer, first in comfort of the memories of childhood and then for my *houshté* (life mate), children, and grandchildren. Then I prayed out of joy and gratitude for the opportunity of being able to share all of this with you.

I can feel the surge of energy through my body. My life is clear and meaningful. There are things to be done, strengths to be gained. This is a time of music and telling stories, for there is much to celebrate. I know that these stories I now share with you are the most important work I have ever done. Now is the time for wholeness. We are healing and we are evolving.

The Ancestors have given us Unity; now it is our challenge to remember. With remembrance we can learn from the legends. The Sacred Circle tells us what all this pain and separation has meant. Now we must remember what the Sacred Circle has revealed. The spiritual quality of thought that we experience will become more intense than anything we have felt before.

There is a deep emotional and sacred tie to these legends and this time in history. These are stories of healing knowledge—stories to ease the heart, and bring understanding to the spirit. The warmth you may feel in the stories is that of the Eternal Flame, burning brightly within you. See the images of the words flow forth.

When you were small you understood that Spirit, by whatever name you called this presence, felt something quite special about you. Now you are coming into the understanding of who you truly are. It is important for us to remember. Embrace humanity's evolution as the stories are recited. No matter what your tradition, pay attention. Be a child at the storyteller's fire. You might be surprised at the recognition that can be found. These stories are related to the events in all our lives.

3

Child of Water and the Origin of Healing

I spent a lot of time evolving the concepts of this project with my special friend JoAnn Lo-n-timi. With her assistance as a friend and helper I honed my skills as a healer and traditional storyteller to a powerful level. I was lucky enough to have this unique friend on my spiritual path, but the time of parting came far too soon with JoAnn's death. The following tale, "Child of Water and the Origin of Healing," was the story that would connect JoAnn, Lynda (my houshté), and me for eternity. This chapter is a healing gift back to my friend—a promise to touch her family always in love. It is also an offering to those of you who knew "Joey," and to anyone who has experienced the loss of a dear friend. I say: Do not deny your feelings as you walk into tomorrow; know that your friend is there, lighting your way. Perhaps the following story will assist you in remembering the eternal link that binds us all, and the infinite source of healing.

The Legend

The people had begun to forget that they were one, All Our Relations. The animals, at first surprised, soon grew angry and sought each other's council.

The Bear Clan met and was presided over by Old Grandmother Bear's son and their chief, Runs in the Light. After several speakers had denounced humanity for its tendencies, war was unanimously decided upon; but Runs in the Light very wisely suggested, "Humans are born with a doorway in the top of their heads through which they communicate with the Giver of All Life. Let it be that from this moment on, for every act of disrespect, this spot will close. Once closed it will only reopen at death to let the true spirit return to the Place of Souls. Walking a path of pure faith may also help a human learn to reopen this connection." And so it was.

The deer also met in council under their chief, Gentle Deer. It was decided that those hunters who slew one of their numbers without demonstrating proper respect and gratitude would be afflicted with an illness—arthritis—that would be born from the fear of scarcity. They gave notice of this decision to the settlement of two-leggeds, and instructed them on how to express gratitude, release the spirit of the slain, and honor and accept the essence as part of themselves.

When a deer was slain, Gentle Deer would run to the spot, bend over the bloodstains, and ask the spirit of the deer if it had heard the prayer of the hunter. If the reply was "yes," all was well and Gentle Deer would depart; if the answer was "no," he would track down the hunter at his lodge and strike him with the fear of scarcity. The rest was left up to the hunter, who had to choose between having faith and being well or becoming a helpless cripple to his fear.

The fishes and the reptiles then held a joint council and arranged to haunt those two-leggeds who tormented them with a fear of death.

Lastly, the birds, insects, and small animals gathered together for a similar purpose with the earthworm presiding over the meeting. Each in turn expressed an opinion, and the consensus was against the two-leggeds. They devised and named various fears that would perpetuate a new life form that would come to be known as disease.

One afternoon as the people were falling into the shadows of despair created by the illusions of fear, Child of Water, second son of Changing Mother and the Giver of All Life, sat watching the drops of rain that collected on the threads of a spider web, making it glisten. As he thought of the people's dilemma, he remembered the temptation he had experienced as a child to poke his finger at the Web of Life.

His brother, Killer of Enemies, had grabbed his hand and made him slowly withdraw his finger. "No," he had told Child of Water. "We must never disturb the flower on its stem, or our sister, Spider, in her web. It is not meant for us to disturb the fragile balance."

Child of Water's forehead furrowed, and his eyes filled with pain. The universe sat on Spider's web, and it had been Killer of Enemies' fear that had initially created the imbalance that now prevailed across the land. His heart felt empty as he now thought of his brother living so far to the north. He sought guidance, calling upon the power of the wind to transport him to the Sacred Lodge. He would seek council from the Holy Parents.

The Sacred Lodge was lit by displays of mystic light when he arrived. The star path he had traveled had swung across the endless dark Medicine Bowl of Eternity that led to the sacred home. The Star Nations spread their wings of light rays and danced in wild delight in the Mystic Garden of Many Moons as he approached.

The Giver of All Life had his son sit on a little patch of the Milky Way and watch the glory of the Mystery spread endlessly. The Fire Dance of the galaxies dazzled with a light show of meteors and meteorites. Shooting stars were hurled across the blue by the unseen hand of spirit forces.

Everybody, everything, every small life force, rejoiced at Child of Water's homecoming. Every day he spent at the Sacred Lodge the trees dropped flowers in his honor and the Thunder Beings sent fire sticks to smudge his Holy Mother. Firelight from the Ancient Ones held the burning stars to light his way. Meteorites skipped, glowed, swooned, and fell to Changing Mother, frenzied by her joy at embracing her child. The Spiral Dance glided in stately rhythm, celebrating his homecoming. Because Child of Water had been away, the sacred space of his heart had been dark. Now the darkness was lifted and the Void of Eternity became radiant in his presence.

Child of Water ran wild, dancing with Earth Mother, skimming over the Milky Way, coaxing everything—every force within space, every speck of consciousness—to open its heart and let the light of All That Is shine through completely and drive the Shadow of Fear from the plane of matter.

The Holy Parents were patient as their son nurtured and healed his soul. They knew of the dark mist that had birthed suspicion in the Third Dimension of Reality. "There is no dishonor in anything that has happened. The responsibility of learning and growing rests in the one who calls the lesson to himself. All will learn. Be grateful and celebrate the worthiness of these actions."

The power of those words hit Child of Water hard and he had to smile. The wind and rain touched his hair, and his smile broadened as the sun broke free and a rainbow filled the patch of blue.

"Ah," a voice said. "The Giver of All Life paints a circle around Changing Mother."

"It is a good omen," Child of Water whispered, his breath seeming to catch in his chest.

"They favor you, so they share their beauty," the voice explained.

They see all things, Child of Water thought as he began his journey back to the village. Walking home seemed like a dream. It was cool and sublimely peaceful. Under the changing late afternoon sky and floating clouds, Child of Water was surrounded by a land where Lizard, Rabbit, Elk, and other relations cohabitated.

As he watched, young Tashiña, daughter of his uncle, Snake, slithered around a rock and saw him. She did not seem threatened by him, and as she paused and looked at him her beautiful markings shimmered in the late afternoon sun.

"Our Father, the Giver of All Life, has said we must remember how to communicate, and Changing Mother has given the Plant Clans a sense of some new and mystical power. I listened and watched from deep sleep," Tashiña hissed. For a few moments, she was motionless, looking at Child of Water. Her tongue flickered. Then she slid gracefully away, disappearing among the rocks.

It was late in the day and the sun was a mammoth red ball behind the western ridge. Tears rolled out of Child of Water's eyes and one hit the corner of his mouth. He sat there, hushed and motionless. He could make out the cliff in the dimming light.

Child of Water rose and walked across the village to his *wickiup* (lodge). He would call a council for the next night to discuss all he had been shown. Tomorrow he would walk in the bright sunshine, enjoying the beauty of a new day. He projected that the sky would be of purest blue, completely cloudless, and the people would feel better with his news. Ah, yes, it would be a good day!

Child of Water entered his lodge to sit and pray. "Grandfather Sun, whose light reveals a million things, you have gone for the day. One by one I turn my senses off; no smell of rose or song of bird to distract my time of silence. I am alone. My memories unleash themselves. Thrilled and throbbing, my heart is aware of the power I have witnessed. A million thoughts and experiences from the light—All That Is—encloses me in my sacred space."

Darkness deepened as Child of Water sat holding the Eternal Flame that burned within. Outwardly he sang a chant. Teardrops and prayers exuded from him. He prayed into the silence, cried his love within the dark. His flame of life burned bright.

"Grandmother Moon, throw your shawl about me. Within your light I come to pray, and be at peace, anytime, anywhere, everywhere."

The next morning, Child of Water awoke to find that two men of the village had become very ill. They became weaker as the day wore on. Tashiña came to his lodge and said, "Why don't you do something for those two men? Why don't you say some words over them?"

Four men among the people just happened to be standing in the Four Directions—one to the east, one to the south, one to the west, and one to the north—as Child of Water emerged from his wickiup.

Child of Water spoke to one of these men, telling him, "Everything is fully awake. Look! Awaken likewise! Our Sacred Father is invisible, yet the energy flows through the rays of sunshine. Fill your veins with the invisible rays; be strong. As Grandfather Sun shines on you and our Sacred Mother, may you feel his rays of protecting love as the dream unfolds. As the light shines always, undisturbed on this land, may you know calmness and strength while you go about your activities and healing. Have strength and learn to share all blessings you receive."

Now this man understood that knowledge was available. Then the four stood in a circle. On the first night the one standing to the east began to chant a prayer all by himself. On the second night the one to the south started to drum and sing snake songs to call the lightning. On the third night the one to the west chanted a prayer. On the fourth night the one to the north began to drum and sing snake songs. They did not conceive this pattern in their own minds; it was shown to them as if in a vision by Tashiña and Child of Water. It was as if the knowledge of what they should chant or sing was suddenly transmitted to them.

Child of Water then said to these four, "Take the power of the Four Directions to the two sick men and make them well." The four men went to where the two sick men were and worked with them, and they were cured. From that time on members of the Animal Clans and the two-leggeds could no longer communicate through common language, but everything brought about by the entity Disease could be cured. The four men became known as Gaan, the four directional mountain spirits, the teachers and guardians of all healing knowledge.

Flower Oracle

As I wrote Child of Water's story I was uncommonly satisfied with the world and my part in it. I smiled to myself as I thought of an experience my houshté, Lynda, had shared in our workshop the day before. She had been sleeping in her tent at the Mt. Hood Sun

Dance in the summer of 1995 when a buzzing had caught her attention. Lynda looked up to see a hummingbird in the top of her dome tent. The hummingbird tried to fly out, but she was either hurt or disoriented. The tiny bird skittered across the tent. Landing at the netted panel, she looked out, unable to pass through the nearly invisible barrier. Lynda tried to help her by opening the netting, but the bird flew off in another direction. She let Lynda come very close, but was unable to understand the actions of the human.

The bird flew from Lynda, but soon became exhausted and landed on the small perch of a seam at the top of the tent. Lynda talked softly, lovingly, to the panicked bird. Moving slowly and constantly speaking in a nurturing tone, Lynda was finally able to approach the stunned, hard-breathing hummingbird and care for her, making a connection through love and compassion. Were all living things so connected?

Yes. At one time the members of the four-legged clans and the winged ones possessed the gift of speech and dwelt happily with the two-legged clan; but humanity multiplied so quickly that the creatures we now call animals were crowded into the forests and deserts, and the old friendship between us and them was soon forgotten.

Irresponsible behavior is not unfamiliar to us. Passivity is equally familiar. In the past, excusing ourselves of all responsibility prevented us from being blamed. We have learned that it has also prevented us from feeling worthy, from fulfilling our potential, from feeling the excitement that comes with achievement. Fear has helped humanity to be irresponsible.

There is a thrill, a racing in my blood, as I share the sacred teaching of the Ancestors. I find myself in awe of the vastness of the healing being offered. I cannot help giving a little sigh of pleasure in the knowledge that we can't fail if we turn our lives over to the higher power of Spirit.

Imagine, if you will, your heart opening into a rose. From its center comes a child. Bring this child out of your body and imagine him or her floating above your head. You are the child; imagine yourself as the child, holding a sun in each hand, while each foot stands on a moon. Hold this image as long as you can.

It's hard to bring out this child. When you try, you realize how many defenses you have built around you—walls of disconnection. You also realize how fear has immobilized you. Some may even doubt that there is a pure and innocent self to bring out anymore. But everyone has one. Everyone must find that child within and bring him or her without, for this child represents the time when our energies were whole and our hearts were untroubled. If you find the child healing occurs, connection is established, and you will be able to fulfill your ultimate potential.

Mystic Marriage

With mordant humor the North showed me that even with my unique upbringing, my conventional perceptions of "work" were limiting my efforts. I am simply not configured to work a nine-to-five day, five days a week. I labor with the flow of energy. I could often be found working hard at two or three in the morning, with a client expected in at nine. The need of the community for my services might be slight at one time and quite substantial at others. By incorporating a more playful attitude into my daily affairs I discovered that the energy I required to accomplish all my tasks could be found within the story of "Mystic Marriage," which reflects the ancestral values that have kept the ever-evolving life philosophy of the Tlish Diyan alive over the last five hundred years.

The Legend

It came to pass that the Tlish Diyan—Snake Clan—sprang from the magical mating of an animal and a human. It happened in a village, in what is now known as Blue House Mesa, in days beyond history's records, far beyond any living memory, deep in the time of legend. The village is now in ruins: the roofs are gone and the hearths are cold. But when it was alive, it was the home of a beautiful maiden, Kaliña, the daughter of a Godiyihgo, an enlightened or holy one. Though beautiful, she had one strange trait: she could not endure the slightest speck of dirt on her clothes or person.

A sacred spring of water lay at the bottom of the mountain. It was known as sacred to Kato'ya and his sister, Tashiña, the rattlesnake twins. Kaliña spent almost all of her time at this spring, washing her clothes and bathing herself over and over. The defilement of these sacred waters—their contamination by the dirt of her apparel and of her person—angered the Snake Twins. They devised a plan to punish her.

When Kaliña next came to the spring she was startled to find a smiling baby boy gurgling and splashing in the water. It was Kato'ya who, like other spirit beings, was able to assume any form at will. The girl looked all around—north, south, east, and west—but saw no trace of a person who might have left the beautiful child.

Whose child can it be? Kaliña wondered. *Only a cruel mother would leave her baby here to die.*

Kaliña talked softly to the child, took him into her arms, and carried him up the hill to her village. There she brought him back into her wickiup, where she lived apart from her family because of her loathing of dust and dirt. As she played with the baby, laughing at his pranks and smiling into his face, he answered in baby fashion with coos and smiles of his own.

Meanwhile her younger sisters had prepared the evening meal and were waiting for her. "Where can she be?" they asked.

"Probably at the spring, as usual!" said their father. "Run down and call her." But the youngest sister could not find Kaliña at the spring so she came home and went to Kaliña's wickiup. There she found the maiden sitting on the floor and playing with the beautiful baby.

On hearing this the father was silent and thoughtful, for he knew that the waters of the spring were sacred. When the rest of the family started out to go see the child, the father called them back, saying, "Do you suppose any real mother would leave her baby in a spring? This is not as simple as it seems." Since the maiden would not leave the child, the family stayed at home and ate without her.

In Kaliña's wickiup the baby began to yawn. Growing drowsy herself, Kaliña put him on the bed and fell asleep beside him. Kaliña's sleep was real, but the baby was just pretending. He lay quietly and then began to lengthen, drawing himself out, extending longer and longer. Slowly Kato'ya, the sacred male snake appeared, like a nightmare come true. He was so huge that he had to coil himself around and around the wickiup, filling it with scaly, gleaming circles. Placing his enormous head near Kaliña's, Kato'ya surrounded her with his coils and finally took his own tail into his mouth.

The night passed, and with it went Kato'ya's anger. He found himself delighted with Kaliña's musings when he had been in the baby's form. And now, as the hours passed, he continued to play these events over and over again in his mind.

In the morning when breakfast was ready and the oldest sister had not come, the others grew impatient. "Now that she has the child nothing else matters to her," the old man said. "A baby is enough to absorb any woman's attention."

But the smallest sister went to Kaliña's wickiup and called to her. Receiving no answer, she pushed the door, first gently and then with all her might. She could not move it and so she became frightened. Running home to where the others were sitting, she cried for help. Everyone except the father rushed out, and pushing together they cracked the door just enough to catch a glimpse of the snake's great scales. They screamed and ran back.

The father, sage that he was, told them quietly, "I expected as much. I thought it was impossible for a woman to be so foolish as to take such a child to her bosom." At Kaliña's wickiup he pushed against the door and called, "Oh Kato'ya, it is I who speak— Godiyihgo 'ishkiñihí. I pray to you, let my child come to me again and I will make atonement for her errors. She is yours; but let her return to her family once more."

Hearing this Kato'ya began to loosen his coils. The whole building and the whole village shook violently, and everyone trembled with fear. At last the maiden awoke and cried piteously for help. As the coils unwound she was able to rise. The great snake bent the folds of his body nearest the doorway so that they formed an arch for her to pass under. She was half stunned by the din of the snake's scales, which rasped against one another like the scraping of flints under the feet of a rapid runner.

Once clear of the writhing mass, Kaliña was away like a deer. Tumbling out of the wickiup she ran to her father's home and threw herself into her mother's arms. But Godiyihgo 'ishkiñihí remained, speaking reverently to the snake. He ended with, "It shall be as I have said; she is yours!"

Godiyihgo 'ishkiñihí and two warrior women of the village called together all the other Diyan, ceremonial leaders, and Chiefs in sacred council. Performing the solemn rites, they prepared feathers, prayer sticks, and offerings of treasure. After four days of ceremonies, old Godiyihgo 'ishkiñihí called his daughter and told her that she must give these things, along with her most precious possession, herself, to Kato'ya. She must leave her people and her home and dwell in the Doorway of the Snake. "Your deeds tell me," said Godiyihgo 'ishkiñihí, "that this has been your desire. For you brought this fate on yourself by acting irresponsibly and using the sacred water for profane purposes."

Kaliña wept and clung to her mother's neck. The girl left her childhood home, shivering in terror. In the center of the ancient village they dressed her in elaborately embroidered sacred buckskin robes and adorned her with earrings, bracelets, beads, and other precious things. Amidst the lamentations of the people, they painted her cheeks with red spots as if for a dance. They made a road of sacred corn pollen toward the distant spring. Four steps toward this spring on the west ground of the village they marked out sacred terraces. When they finished the sacred path Godiyihgo 'ishkiñihí, without one tear, told his daughter to walk out on it and call the snake to come.

At once the door opened and Kato'ya came from Kaliña's wickiup, where he had been waiting. He lowered his head and breast down to the ground in great undulations. He placed his heavy head on the maiden's shoulder, and Godiyihgo 'ishkiñihí said, "It is time."

Slowly, cowering beneath her burden, Kaliña started toward the west. Whenever she staggered with fear and weariness or was about to wander from the path, the snake gently pushed her onward and straightened her course. They went toward the trail and followed it, then crossed Bear Mountain, but still the snake was not completely uncoiled from Kaliña's wickiup. Not until they were past the mountain did his tail emerge.

Suddenly Kato'ya drew himself together and began to assume a new shape. Before long his snake form contracted and shortened until he lifted his head from Kaliña's shoulder and stood up as a beautiful young man in sacred ceremonial dress! He slipped his snake scales, which had grown small, under his flowing mantel. In the snake's hoarse hiss he asked, "Are you tired, girl?" She never replied, but plodded on with her eyes cast down.

In a gentler voice Kato'ya said, "Are you weary, poor maiden?" Rising taller, walking a little behind her, he wrapped his scales more closely in his blanket. He repeated in a softer voice, "Are you weary, poor maiden?"

At first Kaliña dared not look around, although Kato'ya's voice sounded so changed, so kind. Yet she still felt the weight of the snake's head on her shoulder, for she had become used to the heavy burden of guilt and could not tell that the snake's head was gone. At last, however, she turned and saw a splendid, brave, magnificently dressed young man.

"May I walk by your side?" he asked. "Why don't you speak?"

"I am filled with fear and shame," said she.

"Why? What do you fear?"

"I came away from my home with a terrifying creature, and he rested his head upon my shoulder. Even now I feel it there." She lifted her hand to the place where it had been, still fearing that she would find it.

"But I came all the way with you, and I saw no such creature."

She stopped and looked at him. "You came all the way? Then where has the snake gone?" she asked.

Kato'ya smiled and replied, "I know where he has gone."

"Ah, my friend, will he leave me alone now? Will he let me return to my people?"

"No, because he loves you too much."

"Where is the snake?"

"He is here," said the youth, smiling and placing his hands on his heart. "I am he." He drew the shriveled serpent scales out from under his mantle. "I am he and I love you, beautiful Kaliña! Won't you come and stay with me? We will live and love one another, not just for now, but forever. My sister, Tashiña, and I will protect your people."

As they journeyed on Kaliña forgot her sadness. The rocks they climbed to reach the Doorway of the Snake had moss on them; some looked like tawny bones from the previous year's cycle. Fairy dream faces bloomed like fresh flowers in her gaze, for her spirit saw for the first time. But the face that occupied her thoughts most was that of a transcendent beauty, an exquisite charmer who was tender and true. It was a face of sweetness and wisdom, like nothing she had ever seen. This face of beauty was steeped in glory.

She followed her husband into the Doorway of the Snake, and there they lived with the scents of cedar, juniper, sage, rose, and flowers blooming even in the snow. Faces of star beings would come and go; for her there was but one face that could enter the space in her dreams. Smiling love softly gleamed countless silver rays of living beauty, melting their souls into one.

The beauty of millions of cycles did pass. Rainbow rays of beauty kissed lips of laughter and rose petals at dawn. It is the Mystic Couple, glorious and always glowing. In the calm of the pool, where ripples of desire play little games like children, the glimmer of their love still spreads over all. In the mirror of Snake Clan memory, in the crystal pool that is the heart, we see the Mystic Couple's presence there. They are forever part of our blood. As we pass through the door of memories Kato'ya's face is all we see. Flashing feelings, burning vitality, the Eternal Flame, the Stone People, and speaking all melt into one. Vision drawn from pulsating cycles throws its sight to the light, secure in the knowledge of One.

Walking in Balance

There are times when we feel out of harmony with our surroundings, when matters do not go our way and we feel confused and disoriented. Sometimes these moments last a day; sometimes they last for weeks. When we feel like this, we are not integrated with the flow of Spirit.

Being constantly in touch with our higher power is an ideal. There are times of misfortune and discord. When we act without complete consideration of responsibility, we fall out of synch with the energy of All That Is. When this happens we are like birds singing out of tune; we are mired in the discord of illusion.

If we remain patient we can usually ride out these times. We should take action and break the stagnation when an opportunity presents itself. Whether we are waiting or acting we must always try to bring a situation back into balance so we can reconnect to the Spirit, which brings pure joy of heart.

When we connect again we feel relieved. We are back on track, back on target. We learn each time we lose our connection. Sometimes this is enough to prevent the repeating of difficult life lessons, and sometimes it brings hope and faith for the future. Once we know the feeling of the Spirit's unconditional love, we can recognize it again and again and we will not lose faith even in times of fear.

Secret Wisdom

While I was writing "Mystic Marriage," I was treated to dream-memories of one of my childhood teachers, my cousin, Strikes the Enemy. Grandfather had told me once that it was Strikes the Enemy who had taken me out shortly after my birth, out into the canyon where the wind would not pull the breath from my mouth. Then he spoke to me, telling me about my father, my grandfather, and my ancestors—all the things he would tell me again, gradually, as I grew. Strikes the Enemy had said, "Love is that moment that divides the intoxication of life from the awakening. It is the first flame that lights up the inner domain. It is the first magic note plucked on the silver string of the heart. It is that brief moment that unfolds before the soul that chronicles time and reveals to the eyes the deeds of the night, and the work of the conscience. It opens eternity's secrets of the future. It is the seed cast by the Giver of All Life and sown by the Changing Mother, his beloved, brought forth by affection and reaped by the soul. It is the first word. It is love." Strikes the Enemy's wisdom was a part of my life since it began, teaching me, helping me to walk the path, answering my questions. Even though he is gone, I can still feel his essence around me.

When we dream the experience is often deeply involving. Dreams are a form of healing, a way for our minds to recalibrate and adjust themselves. Imagination is a way of projecting our thoughts into believable images that can be contemplated and manifested. We can play with our imagination and use it to inspire creative projects. By cooperating with it we can achieve goals that we never dreamed possible.

I remember everything about the land I grew up on. Lizards and snakes had staked their claim to the hot desert mountains of the North American continent; so had the Apache. Through my cousin's teachings I learned how our clan had come to exist in this land where jackrabbits hopped from one patch of shade to the next.

The canyon that contains the Doorway of the Snake has sheer walls, and with my dreams so fresh the morning that I began to transcribe the legend, I could remember every detail of the land. How the desert gives way to the darker, richer soil, with thickets of aspen and sage lining the way. Sunflowers blooming a brilliant yellow and the red tassel-like flowers of the paintbrush splashing the hillsides. The higher into the mountains, the more the terrain changes. Cedar, yellow pine, pinyon pine, and juniper trees grow in abundance on the canyon rim. A narrow, rocky path opens to a valley off on one side. Sunlight glints off the stream. Chokecherry bushes peek out from among the pines. The air is sweet with the rich smells of pine and cedar. This is where my clan was conceived—on this transitional rift in Changing Mother's terrain.

These pleasant memories often lure me into Dreamtime to reconnect with my source of existence. There, in Dreamtime, Strikes the Enemy joined me.

"Some clans mate for life. Perhaps their love starts with infatuation, passion, and sexual need," Strikes the Enemy said. "Eventually it gives way to a more stable companionship. Not all love survives this transition and lasts, but when it does, partners find a new way of relating to each other. Devoted lovers find that minor flaws can be accepted. At the same time, they find acceptance and companionship in spite of fears and insecurities. Mature love is patient, selfless, generous, and kind. The lover becomes more than the self. In love, we find transcendence and unity."

I wrinkled my nose during this lesson and asked, "But so many speak badly of those they claim to love. Can it be that they really do not know love, or are they bitterly disappointed in themselves? How will I know if I am meant for love?"

"Ultimately your lover is Sacred Spirit, and that sacredness dwells in both you and the partner you will choose. Through love you can come to know the beauty of unity and wholeness. Without Changing Mother, the Giver of All Life would have been static and sterile. Without the Giver of All Life, Changing Mother would have been boundless potential without a catalyst. Through their unification we have found selflessness, purity, and sacredness." Strikes the Enemy picked up a stone person from the path we were walking and carefully examined the markings.

I grinned, and the two of us stayed silent, aware of the surroundings and smells around us. I moved through the trails, which were sometimes so narrow that the rocks rubbed against us. Other times the rocks parted, leaving great paths with only small jutting formations.

He stood a moment and looked over the horizon. Then he pointed off to the left. I looked where he pointed. Baked into the stone outcropping were the tracks of the puma, its trail made up of claw marks.

"Take another direction," he said.

Again we moved through the rocks.

I stopped to smell the desert sage. I saw glimpses of Grandfather in my cousin's face—in his expressions, especially the eyes.

"You need to know the stories," Strikes the Enemy said. "You cannot pass the old ways on to your children if you do not know the stories."

We sat down on a log. I nodded my head in acknowledgment of his words. Strikes the Enemy moved slightly. "It is your duty to continue the Way of the Mountain, to teach your children and others so that the ancient lessons will not be forgotten."

Earth Dragon
and Child of Water

Moving into the energy of the Northeast with the writing of "Earth Dragon and Child of Water," I was literally touched by an angel. I had been taught that all the names for God in different languages and religions are for just one entity. The names and attributes given were truly cultural illusions created for the comfort of individuals confronted with such a presence. Our separation is an illusion. Knowing Spirit is the source of compassion in our lives. We are part of the universality of life. Once we can embrace our oneness we can come to understand the purpose of our uniqueness in relationship to All Our Relations.

How does Spirit look? Look in the mirror or across the table. It's there in every face you see.

The Legend

According to the myths, long ago in Snake's youth he had been one of the two-leggeds' greatest teachers. After the migration to the Doorway of the Snake, he was known for his great power over life and death, he was an invaluable counsel, and he was an invincible guardian of Sacred Earth, Changing Mother. Snake had a son and a daughter. The son, Kato'ya, would carry on the legacy of the Snake Clan through the children he would conceive with his new Coyote Clan wife, Kaliña. Now only Snake's daughter—who some call Tashiña, or Earth Dragon—was without a life mate, and this saddened Snake. He knew his time was at hand and he didn't wish for her to be alone.

Tashiña's voice rode in the winds. Her strength lay in the heart of the Great Mother, and she was well connected to the spirit of the land. She was a beautiful and proud girl. Many young men sent their fathers to Snake with gifts of fine horses and marriage proposals. Among those who desired her for a wife was a young warrior named Tsika, who was the son of the Chief of the two-leggeds. Tsika sent his father again and again to ask for Tashiña's hand, but she would not marry. She would not take a husband until the one who had split apart united with her in journey. She had been in love with Child of Water since the Sacred Parents had placed them together as originators of the healing traditions and keepers of the knowledge.

Much of Child of Water's stamina had vanished after his twin brother, Killer of Enemies, had been sent to the northern polar axis. Child of Water roamed the land for many moons, trying to help his loved ones who had succumbed to the dark mist of ignorance and illness.

One morning Child of Water sat staring out across the meadow.

From the vantage point he had selected he could see many different types of healing plants that would bring comfort to those at home. He rubbed his gritty eyes. He was drained beyond exhaustion.

Child of Water stiffened as he heard the rustle of a bird's wings. The hair on the back of his neck prickled as if stroked by an unseen hand. He knew Tashiña was thinking of him, even as he closed his eyes and made out her face—it was beautiful, with its cute little nose. Her iridescent scales would ripple in the sunlight as she moved.

Around Child of Water were baskets and pouches of herbs and bark; grasses, roots, and berries; each container held its own healing powers. Child of Water felt a sudden, deep aching within. Was there an herb to heal the sorrow that had been created in humanity's soul? Kneeling, he prayed to have the power to heal.

Child of Water knew that Tashiña's eyes were for him alone. She would often search his face, as though measuring his soul. He would often gaze into those eyes, feel the sleekness of her body, the gentle wisps of her breath against his face. Child of Water tried to explain away the fascination as too many days in the desert heat, but he knew it was something else, something brought forth through a thousand cycles. Slowly the feeling of sorrow eased. It was bearable.

Child of Water could feel Tashiña's eyes boring into his. She touched him with such aching gentleness that it set his heart pounding. He saw that the world was being shaken by the Shadow of Fear. He had become well known as a healer, gifting the Sunrise Ceremony from his Sacred Mother to the people. He and Tashiña had made great efforts to extend knowledge of the Healing Ceremony of the Mountain Spirits. The Giver of All Life and Changing Mother, his parents, had instructed him to journey to the southern polar axis to re-establish the balance of the magnetic power between his twin brother, Killer of Enemies, and himself.

When Child of Water returned to the village with this news, Tashiña told him that she would go with him. She put on her best dress of white buckskin, richly decorated with beads, and around her neck she wore a choker of shells. She went to her father, Old Man Snake, and said, "Father, a soft voice echoes from the faraway regions of my soul. I close my eyes and listen. The voice comes to me often. I must travel with Child of Water. Tell me that I can go."

Old Man Snake wept. "You are my daughter," he said, "and I shall miss you. But your mind has long been made up. I see that you must go. Do it quickly. Go and achieve great things with your husband."

Tashiña gathered all of her belongings and rode with Child of Water. As they rode she sang a song: "The essence of my soul rides the mighty wind of Spirit, far from my home I go—to make my life mine, to mingle the dewdrops of another soul with mine, walking a healing way, at last part of One."

Under the sun's gold rays Child of Water and Tashiña sealed their sacred vows and taught each other to fly. There in the blackness of night, shimmering with busy stars, their love was the twinkling of their lights and the waking of the dawn, bursting forth with warm rays born of the heart. In their love they discovered the tiniest eternal spark and joined in the mighty vapor of life, uniting their powerful souls to awaken the clouds and don rainbow ribbons of light.

Then Tashiña got up and walked down from the north. She traveled underground, with Child of Water riding behind her head. As she walked along, the canyon depths rose, and raging waters cut deep gorges, while the Earth Mother labored in birth. She puffed bubbles with her breath, and floated the bubbles on the waves. Tashiña and Child of Water created babbling brooks and the voice of emotional waves as they surged far away to the south, making a great canyon.

In the south Tashiña lay down, and Child of Water lay his head next to his houshté's. "We are home," Child of Water said. "Let us hold on to our laughter and float on clouds of bliss. We will sing with the voices of all and love with the love of All That Is. Your heart is my heart, you soul is joined with my soul, and your most beautiful smile always shall be my smile."

Tashiña and Child of Water had caused different healing herbs to grow along the embankment of the canyons and mountains they created so that we would have the medicines we needed to put right the balance of our bodies. With Killer of Enemies they put right the magnetics of the Sacred Mother, making a comfortable place for all to live.

Becoming Free

Love—so simple, so natural—is such a great challenge in these complex times. Too many other layers of meaning have been super-imposed upon love. Religions straightjacket it, ascetics deny it, romantics glorify it, intellectuals theorize about it, obsessives pervert it. Their actions have nothing to do with love; they come from fanaticism and compulsive behavior.

Love should not be used as leverage, for manipulation, out of selfishness, or for abuse. It should not be grounds for personal compulsion and delusions. Love is an honest reflection of our innermost personalities, and we should ensure that its expression is healthy. Love is something mysterious, sacred, and often the most profound interaction between two beings. Whether what is created is a relationship or a new being, the legacy of both partners will be inherent in their creation. What we put into love determines what we get out of it. Can we actually master the challenge of having open, healthy love?

Lifting the Veil

Today I awoke about an hour before dawn. I felt restless and decided to walk a distance and clear the traces of shadow that fogged my mind. The ability to feel energy shifts within the planetary grid, atmosphere, and combined consciousness of all living things had been part of my childhood training, and at that moment, as I climbed the dirt road up to a small formation of rocks, I was sensing something. I sat down and looked out over the tall grass. Grandfather Sun's wonderful warm fingers tapped on my back. The air was still slightly chilled, and the clarity of the sun and the heat was soporific. A hawk climbed and swooped above me, the undersides of its wings catching a warm current rising from Changing Mother. I watched the bird, its wings outstretched, as it effortlessly glided on the rising river of air.

Compared to the massive movements of the heaven and the earth, compared to the immensity of geological time, the greatest acts of humanity and their monuments can seem so small. We climb the highest mountains, we dive to the depths of the sea, we fling ourselves as close to the sun as we dare, and we are not even on a scale of nature's accomplishments. In our egotism we lose sight of the fact that our lives have the greatest meaning and importance when placed alongside the stars and mountains and rivers. By choosing to live our lives as responsible co-creators, we heal and grasp true reality, which gives us meaning in the context of the universe. If you want to know the force that keeps the sky blue, the stars burning, the mountains high and majestic, the rivers running, the oceans flowing, and love present, then remove the veil of illusion that stands between you and Spirit.

The wind blew.

In this moment I felt a surge of the same energy that has urged me on many times throughout my life. The force that drew me to these mountains east of San Diego is powerful. Something vital for me, for humanity, lies within our Changing Mother.

As I looked up at the mountain beyond, the sight sent chills through my blood. It was as though part of a dream was returning, only I knew I was awake. I was quiet. This strength and freedom was the creation of the great assemblage of all of nature. Thoughts of time gone by flowed freely through my mind. Grandfather spoke of many things when I was small, mainly of the past, how the world had come to be, and how we must adapt. He urged me to learn from him, but I was a child and easily distracted.

I took a deep, deliberate breath and thought some more. Sounds swirled around, but I did not hear; I listened to this silent voice of an Ancient and to those unseen, the spirits of the mountains. I touched a crystal to my heart. I noticed how the mountain was a comforting presence. Everything awaited the unfolding of a vision.

I tried to hang on to the thread of memory about to be unleashed. I took a deep breath and realized the moment was gone. The wind blew, but I did not feel it. I stood and gazed at the sky. I lit some sage and it smoldered, wafting purifying smoke to the heavens.

As I sat on the ground I gazed at the clouds. They gathered themselves into radiance and descended, enfolding me in mist. The mist turned white. I stared up at the clouds, suddenly once again remote in their dwelling place. A hawk swooped down across the sky in a swift arc and then vanished.

"Yes!" I shouted and jumped up. I was aware of the power of this land. Everything we do needs to be imbued with reverence. Reverence comes when we tire of our excesses and find our self-esteem.

Those who contemplate the world come to have a great sense of wonder. The perfection of the stars, the beauty of the mountains and streams, and the invigorating quality of clean ocean air fill us with feelings of celebration. In our own way, we must create our lives each day. We must be responsible and at the same time express the wonder of all that we know as humans.

A painter pauses above a blank canvas. It is not the painting that is as important as that single moment when all things are in a state of potential. Will something beautiful be created? The determination to make something worthy at that moment is reverence.

Kato'ya Dances with the Stars

The Southeast and Ancestors likened my addiction to worry to a measure of spiritual degeneracy. It became clear during the writing of "Kato'ya Dances with the Stars" that my worrying was useless. Questions of inadequacy were being overcome. It was the cancer of emotions, concern gone compulsive. Taking care of myself and doing something nice for those that shared my path helped alleviate and remove this self-created burden.

Now I embrace my power. I act responsibly and am unconcerned. I walk on. There is no worry, because there has been fulfillment. The story was connecting in an ever-sprawling spiral the terms of my identity as a member of the Quero Apache Tlish Diyan legacy. It was an ancient call snaking through me, shifting the way I saw my life.

The Legend

Kato'ya was a fine hunter and a good provider, and he was very much in love with Kaliña. They had three beautiful children and the fourth was soon to be born.

Kaliña had been in labor a long time. The baby wouldn't come out, and it hurt so much that Kaliña cried out. Kato'ya fetched an old healing woman who knew much about such things, and she tried birthing medicines and exercised all her powers. But all her efforts were not enough. The child came out, but Kaliña died.

Kato'ya was crazy with grief. He had loved her so much, and now he didn't know what to do. He ate almost nothing. As he sat weeping beside her grave, he decided to follow her to the Place of Souls. He held all kinds of ceremonies for this purpose.

He made prayer sticks and sprinkled sacred pollen. He took an eagle-down feather and painted it the color of red earth. He waited until sunset for the crack of the universe when the spirit of Kaliña came and sat beside him. She was not sad. She was smiling. His spirit wife told Kato'ya, "From the depths of slumber, as I climb the Sacred Spiral of Wakefulness, I whisper, 'do not weep for me.'"

"You are my food, and when I break my fast of nightly separation I will taste you and say, 'I cannot let you go,'" said Kato'ya.

Kaliña tried to dissuade him, but she could not overcome his determination to be together. So at last she gave in to his wishes, saying, "No matter where I go, the light in my mind will always turn to you, and in the rush of energy my silent cry is, *Follow me. Tie your feather in my hair. If you want to stay with me, you must walk the Star Path of Spirit.*"

At daybreak, as the sun slowly began to light up the world, bathing everything in a soft light and making the yuccas stand out in bold purple relief, Kato'ya tied the red feather to Kaliña's hair. On

the mountains, the vegetation turned gray in color, giving the loom-
ing mounds a mystic shroud, making them seem to float in the air.

The magic mountains hovered over Kato'ya, and the coyotes
howled mournfully, playing on his nerves. Every little desert noise
seemed magnified: the rustle in the cactus of the kangaroo rat, the
scurrying in the sand made by a lizard, the slide of rubble as a rabbit hopped through piles of ancient stone. For a moment, as Kaliña
started to fade from view, Kato'ya felt terribly alone and edgy. The
lighter it became, the more translucent Kaliña became. But the
feather was there. It hovered in midair in front of Kato'ya. Then, as
if caught in a current of air, it began to dance the Coyote's Dance,
moving through the village and into the mountains, leading
Kato'ya ever westward to the Land of Two Lights.

The eagle feather moved effortlessly, floating over the desert
landscape, and Kato'ya had trouble keeping up. He finally called
out, exhausted, "The storms of trials shriek, and worry howls at me.
I work to drown their roar, chanting and praying loudly, 'Kaliña,
wait for me!'"

The small feather stopped and waited. When Kato'ya caught up
they began again. For many days Kato'ya followed Kaliña, and she
stopped every now and then to speak words of encouragement.

One day the path dipped into a deep canyon, and as Kato'ya
reached the top of the cliff the feather drifted away, dancing across
the chasm. Kato'ya called out, "When the night weaves dreams
with threads of memories, then on that sacred tapestry I will paint
scenes of love, forever yours and mine!"

He tried to go down the cliff wall, hoping to climb up the other
side, but it was hard to navigate the unknown path. It seemed that
he would fall into the depths of this canyon of despair to his death.
He almost slipped when a tiny chipmunk scooted up next to him

barking, "In the night, in time of deepest sleep, my dream said to come to you and say, 'Follow me! Follow me! Follow me!'" With his tiny feet the chipmunk danced up the cracks, singing, "My joy comes singing forevermore. New world vision comes about." Kato'ya now followed the Path of Knowledge without any trouble.

On the other side of the canyon Kato'ya found Kaliña waiting, dancing. Again they traveled so quickly he believed his heart would burst. They traveled through the Canyon of Evolution. Waking, eating, traveling, dreaming, sleeping, serving, praying, chanting, and loving as one, their spirits, always singing, were heard by many.

First they passed one lake, then another, until the deep drop at last took them to a third. Kaliña dove into the dark deep water below. Kato'ya knew that a journey on the Star Path must first begin within. He called to Kaliña for guidance that he might be shown the way. The surface of the lake remained like glass in the cool moonlit night.

Kato'ya had walked around the lake for some time trying to find out what to do when he saw a ghost. At first it was like white fog, a mist shaped like a woman. It was Kaliña, calling him: "Call to Star in the night, she will help you. All will be well, the worlds can unite."

Kato'ya followed every instruction. He did everything right. And after four days of crying for clarity of vision his mind began to dance with a star. He saw the bright star coming down the cliff walls and called out, "Cousin, I have waited. Please teach me to dance."

Star descended until Kato'ya could climb on her, and then soared up into the sky.

Kato'ya rejoiced in his newfound freedom as he floated on energy currents that seemed to sweep through time. He inhaled breaths of sage offered from the altars of the human heart, and he cried out his overwhelming sense of joy. The sound resonated a bit too high until he drew it from the very back of his throat. He cried out again, focusing his prayer. "I come from Earth. I come from Sky. I come to this circle, to be all that I can be. I am I. And so it is."

Star swooped down and hovered in front of Kato'ya's face. She wiggled illustratively; Kato'ya followed suit.

"Where is the light that flickered in my life only a moment ago? Where did she go?" he questioned.

"The twilight of many lives has burned between you two. Many lights of love dreams will you meet in your time."

Kato'ya looked down upon Earth. A flock of geese soared over a marsh, and beneath a sagebrush a lizard scampered to a better perspective of the sun's light. Kato'ya heard chanting in the wind: "Kato'ya, from energy unknown come in the silence to transmute magnetic lines."

In chant, the prayer-driven minds found union many times in the bond between two lives. Now the veil of illusion was cast over all but dreaming eyes.

In Kato'ya's search through the Medicine Bowl of All Time broken illusion became a path of direction, a soft focus that penetrated through the twisting veil of ignorance mist. Unborn potential was recognized by the Medicine Bowl of All Time, providing direction and guidance to purified lives.

In the star fire lights, Kato'ya saw all the Ancients twinkling, ablaze in the night sky. Power mingled with unconditional love. And the many lost and searching souls called out to the totality of all life for nurturance. And there, in one connecting glance—a future was revealed, not strictly by chance:

The love that would come would forever restore.
Those times would be sought through birth and death,

> *through life and dreams, and through all the symphonies*
> *found deep within the space of the heart.*

"When harmony was established the universe was carved," Star spoke softly into Kato'ya's vision. "When harmony was fused life did spark. When harmony works in concert with nature, peace rules the heart."

Kato'ya smiled, understanding the crystal purity of energy's great love. In the cloud voice of Thunder he did speak, as rainbow-color flames burst forth from his heart. "I will return to Earth and feed you, my children, wisdom from within. Spirit healing awakens. Your wisdom and love will come again."

And before his eyes he saw his children's forms fade and become transparent. "Seek to set yourselves free to find true identity. Look to the stars, that you might see my image removing illusion, tearing the veil. The promise of tomorrow lies in the Ceremony of the Heart."

Kato'ya then sought to meld himself with One, to share his soul, winding out into the heavens in harmony with all.

Kaliña's ravishing smile—with sparks of joy dancing in her eyes—came to him, making him swoon and enjoy the surge of vitality as they joined.

With This Tear

When sorrow comes, its bitterness soaks everything. The Ancients said that life is an illusion, but does that change the poignancy? Sorrow is a feeling that makes us human. When we gain enlightenment, understanding all life to be a dream, sadness and happiness will fall away.

When faced with a sad situation it is best not to languish in it. We can change things by adjusting our attitudes. To deflect sadness we need only alter its context and allow it to be subsumed back into All That Is.

Dash' shi'heka', I Will Show You Things

"Awake, Naylin 'iskiñihí! Come! You must put your spirit to the wind and follow me! I have things to show you! Now!" The voice was plaintive and high, and in the darkness I awoke, startled and alert. I had briefly fallen asleep and had been dreaming, and yet in dreams comes the voice of vision.

"*Dash' shi'heka'*—I will show you things," said the vision of Naylin Lagé, my great-grandmother. She had appeared to me many times over the last ten years. Her appearance always foretold change of immense proportions in my life.

"Are you ready?" she asked.

"Yes," I said.

"If you are afraid, let that fear go."

I did as I was instructed. Naylin Lagé then said, "Close your eyes and listen to me. Hear only my voice."

I nodded.

"Clear your head. Empty it of all thoughts."

Naylin Lagé sang a song. At first the words were Apache, but then she sang in the ancient language of the Quero. I felt a vibration deep inside me. Spirit flight, or astral projection, is a phenomenon that is hard to explain unless one has had the experience. It starts with a spectacular world of brilliant lights, where one finds oneself in a more powerful reality that defies explanation. Words do not stick to the reality, and reality as we know it seems no more than a distant memory.

The wind grew strong and I heard a rattle; I felt it vibrate to my very core. The haze that had clouded my spirit vision disappeared.

I felt Naylin Lagé's hands on my temples and Kato'ya's spirit entwine with mine. A family of coyotes wanting attention from the big universe let forth some plaintive howls and I was pulled back to the bed I shared with my houshté, a member of the Coyote Clan. Crunching noises came and went. Possibly they were the coyotes I had heard, come to pay their respects.

"Tell me what is in your mind at this moment—what is in your heart," Naylin Lagé said, brushing hair out of my face, as she settled on our bed. "Tell me, Granddaughter. Never fear telling me your feelings. Let us share our thoughts, as we are one being, one spirit. It is destiny that we be together on this night."

The night scene changed beautifully. The unearthly fog lifted. Midnight mist lingered. The stars came out and sparkled like diamonds, and the moon glowed like a topaz. A tear ran down my cheek. My right hand rose and curled around my medicine bag. The corners of my mouth turned upward into a smile. I was not alone. Naylin Lagé was with me, Kato'ya hovered above, and Lynda breathed deeply of Dreamtime. Clearly I heard myself say, "Why are you showing me all of this, Grandmother?"

"Because the time is Now!" retorted Kato'ya.

Naylin Lagé, ignoring my guardian, advised me to trust my inner spirit, which would lend a sense of knowing, a sense of how things would or would not be. She urged me to accept the gift of inner vision. The woman paused, looked straight at me, and said, "When we see pure light streaming down upon us, it is a radiance so bright that we can discern neither details nor hues. But when the light strikes the gossamer wings of a dragonfly or when it shines on the surface of our skin, it is polarized into millions of tiny rainbows. The world explodes with color because all the myriad surfaces and textures fracture the light into innumerable, overlapping dimensions. The same is true of All That Is. That power is pure, and embodies everything. Thus it appears as a void, nothing. Just as pure light has all colors yet shows no color, so too is all existence initially latent and without differentiation in the Source of All Creation. Only when Spirit enters our world does it explode into myriad things. We say that everything owes its existence to All That Is. But really, these things are refracted particles of All That Is."

When the moon was at its brightest, nearly overhead, a strange sensation swept over me. I rubbed my eyes and thanked the Giver of All Life and Changing Mother, all in one breath.

When mixed together, colored light becomes pure, bright light again. That is why many speak of returning to oneness. By unifying all areas of our lives, we unify all distinctions into a whole. There cannot be diversity within unity. When our consciousness rejoins Spirit there is only brightness, and all color disappears.

I sighed again. The evening air had been heady, but the night was nearly over.

"There is more, Granddaughter. Free your mind. The time has come. The sense of wonder has been born in the two-leggeds' souls. They look back to remember," Naylin Lagé said to me. "Kato'ya's promised return reveals the bridge—the bridge that stretches across chaos and allows the two-leggeds to grow in their spiritual light."

My eyes locked with Naylin Lagé's. For a moment I sat motionless, a breeze blowing through the open window. I stared fixedly out at the horizon over which the morning star disappeared. The star and my namesake were gone, and yet they lingered in the fabric of my thoughts, burning at the backs of my eyes.

The prophecies say that the rainbow is the bridge between the heavens and the earth. It has been difficult to walk this bridge. Not only has it seldom appeared, but also we could not easily find it. It seems to be just at the horizon, but the more we move toward it the more it eludes us. To find its end, to even stand at its base and contemplate the dizzying heights that hover over its arc, is even more impossible.

Kato'ya was shown the truth: We are the embodiment of the Eternal Light. We stand where we might see both sides. We will see the Fifth World actualized. We stand upon the Sacred Path of Healing. We raise our vibration so that we may be light enough and pure enough to walk its raindrop surface and embrace our higher purpose.

Snake Children:
The Continuum

The Southwest held compelling truths about family. The narrow ribbon between land and ocean was the perfect place to understand the need for continuance. There I would walk with my houshté and feel the fresh air, share my ramblings, and experience the lulling rhythm of Great Mother's cycles. Walking along the Southwest shore, I was able to attain a sublime sense of purity and peace, content in the continuity of all things. This story was a gift from the Thunder Beings, who are the guiding force of the Southwest.

The Legend

Young people need compassion and guidance. So it was after the crossing of Kaliña and Kato'ya that young Nakía, their oldest son, began to watch his grandmother when she would come to the pool to gather red clover and the sacred datura plant. Nakía followed her back to the village, where close to the family wickiup he transformed himself into a young boy with fine beads about his neck. Then he climbed through the side brush of the wall into the lodge. The family was surprised to see him, but he told his grandmother that his parents had crossed over and that he was too small to raise his younger brothers and sister alone. He remained with the family overnight as the death chant was sung, and the following morning he went home again to check on his siblings.

He arrived and left like that for four days. On the fifth evening he came back, but he did not change his form. He simply slithered into the house and began conversing as usual. Nakía's aunt, waiting for her nephew, said she heard someone talking. She took a light and looked in the place where she heard the voice, and there was a rattlesnake. He shook his head, and she dropped the light and ran.

The next morning Nakía took his grandmother home with him, and there she remained. She raised her daughter's children as if they were her own. Whenever the children saw any two-leggeds from the village they would coil to strike, but their grandmother would say, "No, these are your family. Your father promised safety to the two-legged clan when he took your mother, my daughter, as his wife." And the children would listen.

As the rattlesnake children grew, they also became more curious, and one day they came in from playing and asked their grandmother, "Why did our father take a two-legged as a wife? Two-leggeds are so different."

"Your parents were in love and joined together, one to another, by Spirit's design," she replied. "Many lifetimes ago all creatures lived as one, and then the Shadow of Fear came and stalked the land. This shadow not only twisted the hearts of all creation, but also dimmed the eyes. Only the very faithful could see the true mother, Changing Mother, when they grieved or became afraid."

Nakía nodded at his grandmother's stories of the first trouble. He had seen the burning dark eyes of his aunt when he had gone to get his grandmother, and he had tasted her fear. In the dark shadows lurked something that plagued the land, something he did not quite understand. Did the two-leggeds not see that fear sprang from their search for self-truth and healing?

Life was an enlightening adventure, but most two-leggeds seemed afraid to seek the answers to the questions carried in their hearts. Why? He knew this was not always as it had been.

Nakía knew that for a time he would see his aunt's eyes in his dreams and visions reflecting a gamut of emotion: fear, anger, terror, resentment, and determination. For two-leggeds these were all quite real and too intense an experience.

For a long time the grandmother stayed with the children at the Doorway of the Snake. She taught them the lessons of the Giver of All Life and Changing Mother—the lessons of harmony and peace.

When Nakía reached his prime and was twelve full feet in length, the grandmother said to him, "It is time for me to go back to my husband."

"I will be strong and take care of my family," Nakía said.

"The family is sacred, Nakía. Make it the center of your life. Nurture it, care for it, and give it everything it needs to walk the Sacred Path in a good and right way. You are destined for greatness, Nakía. Look at your family. Feel infinite love for them. Love is powerful. It is the truth that is found in the soul."

The children were sad, but they said nothing until the grandmother started to leave. Then the little girl, Cahokía, ran and caught her by the cave entrance, brought her back inside, and wept because she would miss her grandmother so. But the grandmother kissed her, and suddenly was gone. It was an act of power, Nakía said.

Days after the Snake Children's grandmother had returned to her home in the village, the holy one, Godiyihgo 'ishkiñihí, the Snake

Children's grandfather, stood on the south side of the canyon and stared down the cliff toward the Doorway of the Snake. He had never been this near before, having only visited his daughter in his dreams and visions. From where he stood he could see that the path tapered toward a shallow level rock outcropping in front of the cave.

The trail led into a broken rocky crevice that sloped downward into the cliff. It was a wound, it appeared, that might have been hacked into the cliff by Old Man Thunder. The broken fragments of stone that spilled out of the cleft tumbled near the pool below. The old man began to descend.

About halfway down the trail, something caught his eye to the left and he paused to look. His grandchildren wiggled, crawled in the cave entrance, and disappeared, one after another. He heard them rattle, and then the sounds of their rattles grew fainter, until at last they stopped. A chill caught at him and prickled the hairs on the back of his neck.

The air was still and the pleasant scent of roses drifted across his memory. Sounds of the day were fading, replaced by the sounds of the creatures of the night. A coyote called from a distance—his daughter Kaliña's call?

The old man paused and looked up and down the canyon; the view was magnificent. He dried a few tears that had come with his daughter's precious memory. The beauty of the place made him eager to move on, to meet his grandchildren. He walked on.

The sun was lowering in the west and he hastened to the cave. Standing before the entrance, he called, "Children of Kato'ya, grandchildren of Old Man Yracébûrû, Snake Heart, I honor your ancestors this day. Though they have joined the Silence, I hear their thoughts through the murmur of brooks, the songs of birds, the sound of blowing winds, the beat of drums, and the hum of all vibration."

Stars began to appear in the darkening blue of the sky, and the world was good. Godiyihgo 'ishkiñihí knew there was nothing to do but wait for his grandchildren to appear.

The light faded to the strange bluish-purple of twilight, which distorted not only distance but also reality. There was an air of expectancy, a sense of some spiritual presence. Then the great red disk of the full moon edged its way above the earth's rim to the east and the feeling of enchantment was complete.

The red circle overhead had shrunk to half its size and turned to silver by the time the big head of a giant rattlesnake thrust out of the cave entrance. Nakía's tongue flickered in and out as if in greeting. The old man knew this was his eldest grandson. Then three more big snake heads appeared, and he could sense that these were his other grandchildren. They crawled over his body, hissing at him and looking at him with their snake eyes. While this might have alarmed another two-legged, Godiyihgo 'ishkiñihí was not afraid at all. He calmly let them crawl all over.

The old man's eyes narrowed with thought. "Thank you," he said, "for accepting me as your grandfather. Grandchildren, I have come alone. Our people need your help. They plan to war against those once called brother, the Navajo."

The snakes began a mighty rattling that made Earth Mother tremble. Nakía went back into the hole and reappeared, pushing a medicine bundle before him. "When the clouds of devastation drop rain of fire, we will be with you; you are our family," he said. He addressed them all, but he looked at his grandfather. "In life and death, we are one. This bundle contains the remains of our par-ents—our promise to the two-leggeds that in all life experiences, you can remain in balance. Seek guidance from our father's spirit and realize you are immortal, untouched by the changing condi-tions of the world and life, if you but choose."

Tzégojuñí, the second son, smiled then and spoke: "With myriad thoughts of devotion, we will protect you in awakened silence. We bring the many-colored flames of knowledge for all of faith. They shine with the brilliance of our truth."

A pair of golden eagles flew over and again Godiyihgo 'ishkiñihí felt good, as they were a blessing from the Giver of All Life. The snake children looked at each other with excitement. Cahokía spoke, "The smoke of our prayers for All Our Relations soars with the eagles in spirals to the Sacred Lodge of the Holy Parents—the Giver of All Life and Changing Mother. Let the presence of our father, Kato'ya, glisten in your senses everywhere."

"All words are sung to you in one beating of Earth Mother's heart," said little Mokesh as he looked around the group with pride. "Allow the melody of your feelings to play in tune with the harmony of all love songs, the cry of all tears, the bursting shout of all joy, and the uniqueness of all love."

Godiyihgo 'ishkiñihí heard the eagles' call and looked up. "Grandchildren," said the old man, "know that in the sacred space of our souls, I adore you. I am pleased to receive this bundle. Thank you, my grandchildren."

And so it was that when the people went to find the Navajo, they were nowhere to be found. All returned home unharmed. The two-leggeds were happy, and the old man told them, "Now we must give thanks to my grandchildren."

So all the people went with him to the canyon that was the snakes' home. There he called for his grandchildren to show themselves, and they appeared with much hissing and rattling. The people made offerings of tobacco and good red meat, and the snake children were happy. From then on, they protected the people with powerful snake medicine every time there was a threat of war. And from then on the people were successful in everything they did.

The snakes still help us today. From somewhere deep in the soul, if we listen carefully we can hear the faint voices of the snake children as they pray, "Giver of All Life, may we teach Our Relations to heal the body, to transmute the energy, to heal their minds, to concentrate on smiles and spirit with eternal intuition. *Pinu'u. Daaiina,* I am I. And so it is."

To Tell of Holiness

All the events of my life, the path I walk, and these precious legends came quickly to the forefront of my mind shortly before sunrise one morning in November. I got dressed and walked the dog. For some reason I had been feeling a little down. The deaths of two loved ones had been in my thoughts, even though their times of crossing had been many years earlier.

Death is one of the few givens in life, and yet so many fear it. Society immaturely denies its presence. But it is important to understand death. I have seen much in my life. To do so without coming to understand the meaning of that to which I have been witness would dishonor those I love who have crossed, and deny all my beliefs.

Death is not an ending. It is a transformation. What dies is only a sense of identity, which was only a portion of the whole to begin. Death is a threshold from this life to another.

Undoubtedly the story "Kato'ya Dances with the Stars" had prompted this train of thought. It was beautiful. The very energy it generated had overpowered my senses. I realized something quite drastic was happening to me, as I slowly tried to transcribe the legends of my clan. Each time I applied rational thought to my situation, the realization that I was moving back and forth through dimensions and time jolted me.

I began a prayer of unintelligible words that tumbled from my lips with neither thought nor meaning. I stiffened, throwing my head back and closing my eyes. I felt the energy coursing through my body. As the intensity of my prayer increased, so did my feeling of strength. The sound of faraway drums came crashing into my ears.

Again I remembered the words my great-grandmother, Naylin Lagé, had spoken. I did not understand how it had happened, but I was very happy. Somewhere in these ancient legends there was guidance. I thought of the words, "Death defines the limits of life. Within those limits, there is structure upon which to base one's decisions." Whenever one's life has been fulfilled we must understand that death is only a portal to the next phase of existence.

Following breakfast, I fell into deep contemplation. This brought the vision of Grandfather's back. My grandfather had been slightly less than six feet tall, which was considered tall for an Apache. He had his father's nose and intense look; he'd been very handsome in his youth. As he gazed into my face in that dreaming moment of lucidity his pride and love for me was fully revealed. "Are you all right?" he questioned, as I nodded my head. Tears of joy slipped from my eyes. This had all been planned. My path was one of discovering all that I could be.

The words of our legends are intense within my own being. They are a reflection of my own life's history, a mirror of introspection. I looked up. I felt the earth open to swallow me, but I did not fall. Instead I shot upward and saw the stars exploding around me as I whizzed by them like a comet, faster and faster until the final moment when I seemed to die. The roaring in my head stopping when I floated unfettered, encased in the soundless, tranquil, diamond-studded darkness of space—the world beyond, the abode of All That Is.

A figure appeared, Child of Water, standing with arms upraised. Surrounding him were mystical designs. Then he said, "Finish these legends. These are discipline and wisdom."

When Kato'ya ended a cycle, a new one began. It means the achievement of self-knowledge, discipline, and a new way of understanding self and the world around. It does not stop there, of course. New horizons are always there. Reach out for those new vistas with fresh assurance and wisdom.

"With each turn of Tutuskya, the Sacred Wheel of Life," Child of Water said, "you go further. With each turn of the Wheel, humanity frees itself from the Shadow of Illusion. With each turn of the Wheel comes continuation. Turn the Wheel. Make complete revolutions. Celebrate every turning and persevere with joy."

When I felt myself drifting down I fought it, but I could no longer stay in that dimension. My place was here. I heard sounds again—the traffic on Main Street, the dog's soft breathing as she slept in the back of the car, and Lynda's voice talking to me about her work.

The legends are a gift. I know this. I have been given these stories, this guidance from the Ancient Ones. The cycles of evolution they tell of are real.

I looked around. These mountains I now call home were rich with a variety of shrubs and sage. As Lynda finished cleaning up at her office, I closed my eyes. I thought of the guidance and inspiration I knew to exist within these legends and prophecies of the Quero Apache.

Those who follow the philosophy of the Tlish Diyan believe in using sixteen attributes when interacting with others: honesty, gentleness, patience, noninterference, skill, joy, spiritual love, humility, reflection, restfulness, purity of intent, focused energy to manifest vision, reason, generosity, bravery, and gratitude. We learned these from the Snake Children's actions in caring for our clan. Whenever you need to help another you can also draw upon these qualities.

Notice that self-sacrifice is not included in this list. You do not need to destroy yourself to help another. Your overall obligation is to complete your own journey along the Path of Beauty and Healing. Your example is the best solace you can offer another seeking the path; it is purpose.

Nakia's Destiny

The hospitality of the Northwestern energy, home of the Little Ones who like to take your keys or the spare sock in the dryer, provided the challenge of finding my optimal time of day to work on "Nakia's Destiny." For example, dawn, when it is quiet and the world is fresh, is the best time for me to say my prayers and begin a day swept free of negativity. My optimal time of day to work on this story proved to be around midnight, when worldly cares in the neighborhood had been put aside, rest and relaxation had been established, and the entire world had withdrawn into the nocturnal. It was a time of regeneration as I bathed and immersed myself in the gestating power of the dark and the story.

The Legend

Nakía, oldest son of Kato'ya and Kaliña, was feeling at variance with the world. Wishing to rid himself of the mood, he left the Doorway of the Snake and journeyed to the two-leggeds' village to seek out his mother's father, Godiyihgo 'ishkiñihí. They purified and prayed in the sacred Stone People Lodge together, thanking the Holy Parents for the time they shared. Nakía then thanked Godiyihgo 'ishkiñihí and gave him meat from an animal he had hunted. He left the old man's lodge feeling pure and strong.

The next day Nakía returned to his grandfather's wickiup with more meat. The two ate and talked, and then Nakía left. But he came back often, always with food, for he had never seen any provisions in the old man's wickiup. His grandfather performed healing ceremonies that had been gifted to the people when they still called themselves Quero. Nakía's aunt, Tashiña, and her husband, Child of Water, one of the hero twin sons of Changing Mother and the Giver of All Life, gave them these elaborate ceremonies to drive out the Shadow of Fear.

Nakía grew fascinated with his grandfather's talents. Sometimes as he and Godiyihgo 'ishkiñihí talked, the old man would mix up his medicines or sort through his powerful objects.

One day, Godiyihgo 'ishkiñihí asked Nakía to prepare the sweat lodge, and that was the beginning of a new path for the young snake son of Kato'ya and Kaliña. As he repaired the willow frame and pulled the hides into place, he thought of his actions as a favor to Godiyihgo 'ishkiñihí. He built a great fire and watched the stones as they heated in the coals. He carried water into the sacred purification lodge. He added more wood to the fire. He felt strong and important, and he was glad to help his grandfather. When Godiyihgo 'ishkiñihí and his patient were settled into the lodge, Nakía carried in the large stones. He set them one by one into a depression in the center. Then he stood outside and listened to the water explode with a hiss as his grandfather tossed it onto the stones.

Sometimes when Godiyihgo 'ishkiñihí had to go to a person who was gravely ill he would go into the purification lodge alone to cleanse himself of negative energy. Nakía would hold Godiyihgo 'ishkiñihí's medicine blanket while listening to the old man sing and pray. He had taken to accompanying Godiyihgo 'ishkiñihí to the sick person's wickiup, carrying his healing paraphernalia. Godiyihgo 'ishkiñihí would clear the wickiup and step inside. Nakía would wait outside for however long it took, listening to the singing, the prayers, the rattles, and the eagle-bone whistle. Often these healings took all day, sometimes more. Eventually Nakía's grandmother would bring food for them to eat and ask if they needed anything.

Later in Godiyihgo 'ishkiñihí's wickiup, as his grandmother tended the fire, Nakía would watch his exhausted grandfather sleep fitfully and wonder at his power. But the young snake-man had no thought to possess such knowledge. He was just happy to help.

The sun ascended toward the zenith of the sky. The mountain rose with a mist around it; it seemed to glow and glimmer, to be illusory and unsubstantial. The essence of the energy surrounded and enfolded Nakía, extending away, vague and dreamlike and spectral. It was magical to watch Godiyihgo 'ishkiñihí sort through his healing tools. He said to Nakía, "Your father came to me last night as the evening coolness settled on the land. Mist rose from the pond, twining its phantom arms into the twilight sky. The somber shadows of rocks and brush melted under the deepening blanket of darkness, smoothing until they pooled with the night, the croaking of frogs, and the hum of insect wings."

Nakía listened intently to his grandfather sharing the vision he had the night before. He tried to fight the heaviness of his eyelids, but the magic of the moment eventually overcame him. Images danced on the back of Nakía's lids, flickering orange and blue as the trance state numbed his body and coiled through his thoughts.

Nakía's next sensation was of unimaginable blinding light, hot and searing. The light penetrated his body in a thousand slivers, piercing clean through his spirit.

Nakía's thoughts were disjointed at first, forming like crystals of ice on a pinyon pine. "What is happening to me?"

"You asked for direction," Kato'ya's voice answered from a great distance.

"Father . . . Where am I?" Time passed rapidly.

"Hovering between Shadow and Real World. Light gives birth through dreams. Here all of time—past, present and future—exists, never ending. Remember that, Nakía."

Nakía's gut tightened as he fell through nothingness. He spun, weightless and out of control. He tried to find balance.

"Relax," a voice spoke softly.

Nakía relaxed, lifted his head, and looked into a face framed with brown hair and possessing eyes that glistened. A child of about eight years old looked lovingly upon him.

"Things work differently here, Nakía. This is the Real World where illusions no longer veil your thoughts. I am Naylin 'iskiñihí. Kato'ya has sent me. Come, there is not much time."

Nakía became aware of a road stretching before them. It tied together the earth and the heavens with a broad band of rainbow colors.

The child gazed upon Nakía and said, "Your parents have heard the cries of your soul, and have sent me here to comfort you. Open your heart and I will share your future of light. Ask and I shall show you the Path of Truth."

Nakía complied with her bidding, and asked, "Who am I, Spirit, and what is my purpose in this world shadowed in fear? What are these mighty hopes, these mountains of lessons, and these strange events that keep us from the Sacred Parents? What are these thoughts that come and go like a flock of doves? What are these prayers and stories that we compose with desire and joy? What are these sorrowful and joyous conclusions that embrace my soul, and yet are oblivious to my grief? What are these voices that lament the passing of my days and chant the praises of my childhood? What is this force that moves me, and to what unknown destiny? Tell me, Spirit, what are these things?"

The child opened her lips and spoke, "You, Nakía, would see the world with the eyes of the Giver of All Life. The circle will come full; it's time to see."

Around Nakía brilliant stars twinkled like frost, while darkness flooded outward, rippling in the farthest reaches of the sky.

"Go into the field and see how bees hover over the sweet flowers and the eagle swoops down on its prey. Go into your neighbor's wickiup and see the infant child bewitched by the firelight and let the mother be. All that you see was and will be."

A passageway seemed to open in the air at the end of the path, allowing Nakía to glimpse life scenes as they appeared on Changing Mother.

"The many lessons, dreams, strange events, and lovely thoughts around you are the spirits that have been and yet will be. The prayers and stories your voice utters are the strands in the web that connects you and all others. The sorrowful and joyful conclusions are the seeds sown by the past in the field of your soul, to be reaped by the future."

Nakía closed his eyes and softly sang a chant, reassuring himself that all would be well.

She continued, "A youth will toy with your desires and open the gate of your heart for love to enter. Changing Mother, Earth, is the redeemer of souls, freeing them from the bondage of self-created illusion."

As if they had exchanged souls for the briefest of moments, Nakía saw himself through the child's eyes. He felt his heart flutter wildly in the cage of his chest, and the moment ended.

"The world that moves with you is your heart, which is the world itself. And all who exist on the physical plane, which you call Mother, are the messengers of the Giver of All Life, who have come to learn the joy of life through lessons and to gain knowledge from seeing through illusion."

The child laid a hand on Nakía's burning brow and a thread of trust was built between them, strengthening each moment, until the child's voice echoed all around Nakía. "Come with me. Do not hesitate. To go forward is to move toward your destiny of perfect light. Know I love you and will be with you always. Walk the path and fear not the exchange of lessons."

Nakía squinted, as the child, with a puff of clouds, grew wings. Twirling in a sacred dance that bore them both up above the mountains, she beckoned and pointed behind her. Nakía looked back and saw a strange world from which rose dark smoke of many hues moving slowly like phantoms. A thin cloud almost hid a magnificent city from his gaze.

Even from the distance, Nakía could see many confusing sights. After a moment of silence he exclaimed, "What is this I see, Spirit?"

"This is the Fourth World of Separation as it shall unfold."

And Nakía gazed upon this wonderful scene, where he saw many objects and sights: large buildings made for action, standing giantlike beneath the wings of slumber; *kivas* (chambers) of talk around which hovered spirits at once crying in despair and singing songs of hope. Nakía saw medicine wheels built by faith and destroyed by doubt. He spied towers of thought, lifting their spires like upraised arms of beggars. He saw avenues of desire stretching like rivers through valleys; storehouses of secrets guarded by sentinels of concealment and pillaged by thieves of disclosure; towers of strength raised by valor and diminished by fear; shrines of dreams, embellished by slumber and destroyed by wakefulness; temples of solitude and self-denial; universities of learning lit by intelligence and darkened by ignorance; taverns of love where lovers became drunk and mocked one another; theaters upon whose boards life acted out its play and death rounded out life's tragedies.

Such was the world from far away, though in reality nearly visible through the dark clouds.

"They lost their spiritual connection." The child let out a taut breath, then beckoned to Nakía and said, "Follow me. We must go."

Tears blurred Nakía's eyes as the scene disappeared. "Where are we going, Spirit?"

She said, "We are going to see your father."

Nakía wiped at his eyes and nodded. He felt desperately tired. It seemed that it took every ounce of strength he had remaining to follow Naylin 'iskiñihí.

The path before Nakía changed, glittering like a million great wings before fading into a new scene. A distant ancient drum revealed itself as Nakía's pounding heart. When Nakía gazed into his father's brilliant eyes he felt the great snake's power, so shrouded in mysterious secrecy. Images filled his mind, images of a time when all would be as the Sacred Parents had intended it to be.

The images he saw reflected in his father's golden eyes drew Nakía irresistibly, as if they pulled at his soul. "A time will come, my son, when all will dream and be awakened to their true identities.

They will embrace a belief system that will move and change with the magnetics of evolution.

"The Ancestors will be praised. And our descendants cherished. The promise of the Giver of All Life's blessing is upon all. In this time, life will be bountiful for all, and hunger will remain no more.

"The spirits always hear our words. The spirits of all Ancestors speak of a time where there is no time. This shall be the Fifth World of Peace and Illumination.

"Energy is like smoke; stir a part of the smoke and the other tendrils are affected. All will come to understand, at the end of the time known as the Fourth World, that to enter the light they must learn what they need to do to maintain life's balance.

"The separation of this world is limited. Many will be caught for a time in struggles they can't comprehend. The time of separation was necessary. But another time is coming. You must be patient and strong. You have been chosen.

"Unite the worlds within yourself and become who you are. I will direct you. When the time is at hand, I will return in the stars. Remember, no matter what, do not fear the change. You will receive my power and lead. You are Snake Clan—proud, strong, and spiritual. Sacred. Our purpose has been instilled into your very being.

"You are Nakía. You will show all what it means to be magnetically balanced with Changing Mother."

Nakía thanked his father, and as he turned to leave he thought of the images he had seen of his future and the future of the world. His father was watching him with a look of profound respect.

"By the way," called Kato'ya, "when I appear in the stars—when I return in the night—lie on your left side to sleep. It will ease the process. Dream of all that has happened here. You and those who know will possess the magic it will take. You will fear nothing, and the world will be filled with illumination and peace."

Something then grabbed Nakía from nothingness and squeezed him. Fingers worked along his muscles, squeezing, prodding, massaging. He smelled antelope meat. He flipped over in the air and whirled around, choking. The hands were powerful. They seized Nakía and brought him back into his body from his journey through the vast blue sky like a blazing meteor. When he opened his eyes, Godiyihgo 'ishkiñihí was there.

The old man smiled at Nakía, his heart in his eyes. No exchange was necessary as the two eagerly joined in prayer: "The bells of Nature's harmony, the drumbeats of our hearts, the myriad minds and chants, flowers from the garden of souls, and the scent of sage are gathered within our souls, within this place. With eyes open we call to you with chants, devotion, activity, and wisdom; with love, heart whispers, tearless tears of connection, and with silent joyful intuition.

"No more are you unknown to us; during our celebrations of joy we look through infinite starry eyes into the Mystic Heart. With the sighing wind we mix our prayers. Our chants sing with our beating hearts. We feel the Mother's beating in all hearts. We watch Spirit working in gravitation and other forces. In the sound of footsteps of All Our Relations we hear the call of love and we are grateful.

"We are Children of the Universe and co-creators of our world. No more are we blind; now we see. And so it is."

Flight of Kelei, the Hawk

Achieving my destiny was a matter of trusting and embracing the pattern of my life.

I waited patiently. I watched as a hawk soared upon the wind from beyond the top of the mountain. Its wings were incredibly wide. This creature stroked across the sky and hung there, motionless, balancing on the wind. I looked up. I stared in awe and introspective silence. The symbol of Spirit's message had been with us since Lynda and I had moved to San Diego. To see it again, soaring in holy reverence, was another special omen.

The hawk was banking again, dipping its wings, catching a thermal updraft, rising with it, circling, touching each of the sacred directions of the universe that gave birth to the Winds of Change. Then it veered away. I stood on the balls of my feet, reaching with all my strength to where the hawk had disappeared over the horizon.

There are so many secretly treasured spiritual paths. They all share the same mystical sense of communion with the Divine. This sense of connection is not something peculiar to one culture. I nodded solemnly as I thought about this.

All cultures know a mystical core that emphasizes continuing remembrance, devotion, and connection with the totality of All That Is. They call it by different names. But what does it matter what people call it? When they discover the piece of themselves that is holy they describe it according to their history and culture, but they all discover the same thing: There is only one Divine Source in life.

I reached into my medicine pouch and took out my bandanna. Placing it around my head, I touched the medicine bag at my neck. It held the wonders of the universe over my heart. For generations mystics of all traditions have plunged into the higher consciousness. When they have met on the unspeakable dimensions they have known, without verbiage, that they have reached the same core of spirituality. No matter where in the world one may be, there are traditions with the purity to lead to true identity.

Facing the East, I held up my arms and prayed for several minutes to the Giver of All Life. Then I asked Changing Mother to grant me guidance and vision.

I called out to the spirits in prayer, thanking them for providing yet another beautiful day of life.

I heard the voice, high and compelling: "Come." I heard the voice carried on the wind, pulling at me. I looked at the sky. Clouds drifted across Grandfather Sun, blocking his light for a brief moment.

"Come, Little One. I have come for you." I heard the voice, the breath of the wind, and I concentrated on it. "Close your eyes. Come with me," she said inside my head. "I have something to show you."

I did as she said. Immediately I felt the comfort and security of her close by. Strange as it might seem to those who are still searching to experience the magic of All That Is, this was a realm in which I felt content.

"I'm ready, Kelei."

The leaves fluttered as the wind whirled and tiny spirals of dust spun on the ground, picking up fallen leaves and wisps of grass.

Had the hawk spoken again, or was it only the wind?

I stretched out my arms, palms up, my hair blowing behind me. I heard a song in my head. I opened my eyes and there in the sunlight, I watched Kelei, the hawk, come to rest on a rock. My body tingled, and I drew in a deep breath before closing my eyes again.

"Take me with you, Kelei. Give me flight."

The sensation began at my feet and then traveled up through my body. I raised my arms upward to the sky, and in a moment I knew a transformation had taken place.

"Do you see?" Kelei asked.

"Yes," I answered, understanding why she had taken me on this flight. One's life destiny is not easily revealed. It's too big. Grandfather and other Elders had foretold my life since I was small, but I was given glimpses, pieces of the whole as my true purpose continued—and continues—to be clarified. As it has come together, there has been a tremendous feeling of assurance with each piece of the puzzle gained. A sense of reverence overwhelmed me.

"You are part of this story," Kelei said softly.

Suddenly light exploded about me, showering me with sparkling multicolored lights, sending me floating toward Changing Mother upon an iridescent rainbow.

The descent was slow and gentle, a light, airy mist of rapture, and in a moment I was back on the ground. I heard a voice as I caught a glimpse of the hawk's filmy shape, a translucent form that shimmered in the sun's shadow.

"It will all become clear to you," she said. "Do what you must when the time comes. Have no fear for yourself. The magic is in you. Follow your heart. The spirits of your Ancestors rest there."

I watched as she faded into the light. She knew what would transpire during this time of Passing Power—this time of transition between the Fourth World of Seperation and the Fifth World of Peace and Illumination—whereas I could only speculate. Nakía and I were connected. Our souls were connected. Kato'ya had been my guide my entire life, and he was a guide that I had been given by my grandfather. But now it was Nakía's time.

I understood the hawk's message. What she had shown me would soon have great significance, as would everything that had come to pass in my life. A quick breeze—the beating of her wings—told me she was gone.

I felt a beautiful, total peace in the moment. Crystal tears escaped my eyes. The sweet scent of sage filled my senses.

"You are pleased with yourself," Naylin Lagé, my long gone great-grandmother, called out.

"Yes," I replied. "I guess the importance of this time causes the feelings. I can't help it. My path has not always been easy and I realize this is because I tried to run from it. There was doubt." I stopped and looked into the dark shadows that were a vision of her eyes.

"Because you are mixed blood."

"All I want to do is what Spirit would have of me."

For a long moment the image of my ancestor stood unmoving. The wind combed through her hair and ruffled the fabric of her shirt. Then, as if in a trance she curled her right hand around the small medicine pouch she wore around her neck. When Itzá, the eagle, swooped down out of the sky to alight next to her, she did not seem to notice, even though the bird was more than half her size. She said, "You live honorably; there is no failure. The Thirteen Sacred Mirrors of Fire are in progress. Kato'ya has returned to pass his power to Nakía, and so too your grandfather to you. This time will awaken all that is good among humanity and within you. You are connected to this mystical force that has been part of our lineage since time beyond beginning. You must share the stories, dreams, gratitude, and good thoughts you carry. It is the celebration that feeds Changing Mother and keeps the Universal Force forever strong. You are guardian of Kato'ya and Nakía's continuing legacy, just as they are guardians of humanity.

"I say this because it is truth. The omens have always been strong for you, Naylin 'iskiñihí. Let us sit."

As I sat I concentrated on the clouds in the sky. The wind howled so hard it blew the clouds around the universe. The sun sailed through the day. The wind lifted ebony strands from Naylin Lagé's shoulders. A tear sparkled in her dark eyes. I was still for a long time.

I knew the visions of Spirit, feeling a oneness with All My Relations. It was like I had returned home.

I listened. I stared into the clouds. The sensations danced. Their melding held me spellbound and my mind slipped back. I blinked as if awakened from a dream.

I held my breath.

I sat in stunned silence. I paid attention. I knew I need have no fear. Not in this place and time. The spirits of my ancestors were here with me.

Naylin Lagé looked up. "I must leave," she said. "Others share the vision and will find you." Pleased by a sudden memory she smiled and sighed wistfully, a woman's expression of longing for things that nurture the heart. "The central law of the universe is breath." Her smile vanished. "Without breath, there is no life."

"The complexity of this principle is great indeed, Grandmother."

"You breathe; that brings you oxygen. You breathe; that sustains you. You breathe; that regulates your heartbeat, feeds your brain, and makes your blood red. Remember that."

For a time neither of us spoke. Naylin Lagé squinted at me.

"Deeper still: You breathe and the entire energy field of your body is sustained and set into motion. When that field, so intimately tied to breathing, is integrated with your mind you have the power of spirituality."

I gave the holy woman a proud and level glance. Breathe. I thought of all the people I had told to slow down and breathe recently.

"Just as you breathe, so too does the universe breathe. In fact, you can think of the entirety of life as breath. When the world breathes, all things are sustained. Weather moves as it should."

After a moment she continued. "Plants grow as they should. Animals are made strong. The very forces of Changing Mother are set into motion. And together a mighty field of energy is generated, a much larger version of what happens in your own body. Connected to that field is a universal mind." She gestured to me.

I rose. Now as I came to face my Ancestor beaming at me with glowing eyes, I listened to the drum of Changing Mother in my heart.

Do you want to know the secret of being spiritual? Breathe. . . .

Tzegojuñí, the Shapeshifter

"Tzegojuñí, the Shapeshifter" came directly from Spirit above. This story revealed depth immeasurable, and its power has touched all who have read it. It was an affirmation for myself and a prayer that society's understanding would not be incomparable to its vastness. I trust the overwhelming power of Spirit in the need to present rare insight into a complex question of acceptance.

The Legend

The second-born son of Kato'ya and Kaliña went through a change of spirit as a result of dreams he experienced.

Tzegojuñí was a master of the art of camouflage. He was able to disguise himself with dirt and plants so effectively that he was virtually invisible until you were right on top of him. Tzegojuñí was at home here, traveling through this rough terrain. He had a power to be reckoned with and was shown great respect in the early times of this sacred land.

In the dimness of the Doorway of the Snake the children of Kato'ya and Kaliña slept. Tzegojuñí should have been asleep, but unease nagged at him. He stared up at the dark cavern roof and listened to his brothers and sister breathe softly as they slept. He could hear a dog barking somewhere. The animal sounded distant, so he knew it was from the two-legged village.

Sleep had not provided rest for several nights. Spirit dreams called to him in the night. Tzegojuñí remembered a little but doubted he would recall everything. The night air smelled of water, damp earth, and summer flowers. The growing moon angled light over the canyon. The soft rhythms of the night soothed him.

The moon, a shining crescent, hung over the eastern horizon. Tzegojuñí gazed at the thousands of stars that dusted the heavens. Tomorrow he would discuss his dreams with his elder brother, Nakía. Nakía was hereditary Clan Leader, and when their father returned from the stars, the power Kato'ya possessed would pass to Nakía. Already he had grown into a wise and spiritual snake-man, and would know how to advise Tzegojuñí.

When Tzegojuñí told his dream to Nakía, the elder brother grew silent. He smoked a long time. He smoked far into the night. Sometimes he'd appear frozen in spirit flight while other times he hummed, but always he would return to his smoking. Finally he tapped the pipe out and told Tzegojuñí to go to sleep; he would prepare the Stone People Lodge in the morning.

After their purifying sweat, Nakía led Tzegojuñí to a small cavern in the back of their cave home. He made his younger brother lie down and pretend to sleep. He took a datura root and dropped it into the boiling water over the fire. After a while he dipped a bowlful and passed it under the nose of Tzegojuñí, making his brother inhale the sharp steam. Nakía then pounded some sage leaves and snakeroot in a wooden bowl. All the while he chanted and sang purifying songs. When the mixture had been pounded into paste he dipped his fingers into the pot of boiling water, scooped the paste onto his fingertips, and then placed them on Tzegojuñí's body. The younger brother flinched, but the steady pressure of Nakía's hands against him made him relax. Four times Nakía applied the compound. Then Tzegojuñí slept, and while he was sleeping Nakía pulled an eagle wing from his parfleche (rawhide case). He made motions of the eagle flying with his hands, then he struck the younger snake-man with the wing. As he burned some pinyon and passed it over the body, he sang the purifying song, the gentle hissing of their father. Finally he blew several shrill notes over his brother with his medicine whistle, and dripped blue paint from the end of it onto the forehead of Tzegojuñí. Nakía fell back and said, "It is done."

When Tzegojuñí awoke, he felt that he had been to another world and returned. He propped himself up and he felt light and free. A voice nearby entered his ears. "Tomorrow you must go and meet with the spirits. They will complete the Ceremony of the Shapeshifter."

Tzegojuñí looked across the fire and saw the sky-blue eyes of his older brother. It was night.

The next morning the young man sat alone, staring up at the snake bundle, which hung from a tripod. It was a small bundle. He had decided to sit there alone before his quest, looking at the bundle and speaking to the spirit within, the spirit of his father. Nakía had kept the bundle since the crossing of their grandfather, Godiyihgo 'ishkiñihí. Tzegojuñí knew that once he completed his journey the bundle would be passed to him. His brother had been waiting until Tzegojuñí was ready and had experienced the dream that would forever change Tzegojuñí's life. All the living things of All That Is had given their blessings to the medicine power that would be birthed. The power was immense. But to birth it, everything must be done right.

The beat of the drums had been incessant since shortly before Tzegojuñí had begun his prayers. As he entered the light of the canyon, the Coyote, Libaye, whirled and danced around the fire as he blew madly upon an eagle bone whistle and beat his drum with a hide-wrapped stick, all the while performing a series of clever mimes designed to prompt those who watched him into guessing the identities of the relations he was impersonating.

"Snake!"

"Buffalo!"

"Eagle!"

"Bear!"

Whenever a correct answer was given Libaye would leap straight into the air and shake his bottom. The young ones squealed and the audience clapped their hands and laughed with pure pleasure.

They laughed easily and applauded vigorously, urging Libaye to continue the game until he at last feigned an enormous swoon and fell on his back, legs up, squawking like a crow. Young ones broke from the circle to swarm all over him, tickling him. When he was reasonably sure every little one had counted coup (celebrated victory) he scooped up an armload of giggling toddlers and rose, bowing mightily to his audience.

Tzegojuñí smiled, thinking of the future of this land, a place for the little ones. Those relations were here to support his quest. He was being washed in the breath of their love. As he let his mind wander, the beat of the drums turned to the monotonous tones of the singers, and the Mountain Spirit Dancers moved through variations of the ceremony. They danced for hours, the painted colors of their bodies casting off different hues in the bright sunlight. It was one of the chajala, or healing dances, the most powerful of medicines. Leading it was Nakía.

Tzegojuñí's own power had been enhanced only a few months earlier when he had been struck by lightening, and this power was apparent by an amulet he wore constantly around his neck. Spear-shaped and made from fused quartz, the talisman came from the base of a pine tree.

The drums were suspended above the earth, from upright posts of concentrically arranged poles. The Thunder Drums were great six-foot circles of bent willow over which skin had been stretched taut then warmed over sacred fires until all the moisture had been removed.

Next to Tzegojuñí sat his sister, Cahokía. She had their mother's nose, intense look, and beauty. "You have great power," Cahokía said proudly to her brother. "Never in memory has one ever done this. When you were young Nakía says you went on spirit flights with Eagle. You have always been powerful. Now you will be respected above all. You are almost as sacred as Father."

Suddenly Nakía darted from the fire to Tzegojuñí, chanting loudly. He held a four-strand medicine cord high and sprinkled liberal amounts of pollen over Tzegojuñí's head. Then Nakía stopped abruptly and the music ceased with him. The dancers froze and all eyes were on Nakía.

Sprinkling pollen toward Tzegojuñí from several feet away, Nakía chanted in the language of the Ancient Ones, the Quero, and turned back to the Mountain Spirit Dancers. Each began dancing energetically to the beat of the drums and the chant of the singers; each was naked to the waist and wearing fringed buckskin kilts and elaborately decorated moccasins to the knees. On the head of each was a mask, and atop the masks were headdresses.

The sun lit their twisting bodies and reflected from the eyes of those who sat away from the dancers, watching solemnly and lending their voices to the chanting. As the volume of the music rose, the dancers' pace became more frenzied. They jumped about the circle, muttering, singing, leaping, swaying, whirling, and building the energy to a great crescendo.

Faces danced before Tzegojuñí. And then utter silence.

With a sigh Tzegojuñí followed Nakía to the foot of a high cliff. "There is a special cave that Tzegojuñí must visit. Our father, Kato'ya, has told him to go to this sheer cliff wall and climb it, then pray to the Giver of All Life."

"But that is impossible!" the people cried out.

"I will do as my father commands," Tzegojuñí replied. "Stay at the foot and pray for me." And they watched him go to the base of the cliff, where he shifted his balance and prayed fervently. Then he took his first step, finding a hold and then another and another. Twice he slipped, almost falling, but he continued upward. Now and then it seemed that he could go no farther, but he always found one more bush, one more rock to help him climb.

Suddenly an opening appeared in the solid rock and he went inside. Tzegojuñí spoke a prayer to all the Above Ones, thanking them for his safe climb, then he heard a quiet voice, a deep voice. "The journey home has begun. In the kind eyes of all, notice the sparks of mercy. Dark lives flicker with small lights of life. The journey home will be slow through the sand storms of despondency. Yet the glimpse of hope will arouse humanity's efforts. Touch your thirsty lips and drink deeply from the well of faith and bliss." Tzegojuñí found himself looking into the face of Grandmother Bear.

He looked into the weathered face of that giant grizzly and tried to read the emotions there. While her mouth appeared to smile, her eyes had become wet. It was as though Grandmother Bear greeted him both fondly and sadly. There was something else there, something in the way the Great One trembled, as if she wanted to say something more. Tzegojuñí remembered the reason given for the separation of All the Relations, and now he wondered if some part of Grandmother Bear not only understood that reason but also had condoned it. The search for a path back to the Sacred Parents was an effort to strengthen the final connection for all. It had been determined by All That Is.

With the soft touches of his spirit, Tzegojuñí tuned his intuition. As he moved on further into the cave he caught another voice—a sweet harmony, the strains of his singing heart, the chorus of agelong cravings for true understanding—caught within his soul. He kept improving his perception as he walked farther into the darkness, waiting to catch the next voice.

With infinite patience he kept on, listening as he went, and just as he almost gave up he encountered a puma, whose voice gushed through his heart. "The lands of the mind lie clogged with the dirt of delusion. You will bring sweet showers of healing to wash the land of spiritual carelessness. In your mercy the cruelty of ignorance shall drown. Your love will bathe thoughts with wisdom.

"Scatter roses of love on your life path. By inhaling the fragrant blossoms your relations will hasten their footsteps to the Lodge of Knowledge." Tzegojuñí saw the look of hope in the great cat's golden eyes. Tzegojuñí looked up and saw figures on the walls of the cavern passage, a sacred passage, and he looked again at the face of the puma. He realized there were things he was not old enough or experienced enough to fully understand. He told Puma of his mission and the guardian seemed to approve of Tzegojuñí's vow. There was no other who had ever made such a vow, so he would be made Sacred if the ceremony were successful.

"There is one more guardian before you reach your destination,

Tzegojuñí. Your father and I spent much time discussing the father of the world. He is a great one." Tzegojuñí looked around at the pictographs and beyond them. He saw the passage enshrouded in darkness. "Yes," he said.

The next leg of the passage was cold. Tzegojuñí's mind wandered as he traveled. In the silence he held his breath, waiting and listening. Purple tints began to appear like a mist on the floor, casting irregular patterns against the luminous walls.

High above a streak of light burned greenish as something flew across the ceiling. Taking one last breath Tzegojuñí followed the streak of light.

Had the cavern not been so still he never would have heard the soft whisper. From some great distance a voice murmured, "In the Cave of the Dragon, the ore of your life will be smelt. The fire of experience will melt everything in you. The Eternal Flame will burn away all the fear within you; it brings you clarity and through love transports you into peace. You are the Arrow of Truth you so proudly display at your throat, a symbol of compassion and honesty tempered by a balance of male and female. With a harmonious mind always remember Sacred Law."

The words walked across Tzegojuñí's soul. His teeth gritted and groaned against each other as he held his breath in silence. He tipped his head back to peer up. Crimson light reached across the space to stroke him. It was his mother's loving gesture.

Then Tzegojuñí's mind went black and he thought he felt his shadow slipping away. It was peaceful. He felt his body grow warm and cold at the same time. Then he was flying over the land. He saw many swimming happily in the waters of apathy. Others had fallen into complacency and self-deception. They fluttered in sadness, choked with indifference, and finally crossed into the Sacred Breath of All That Is to discover the illusion of it all. Tzegojuñí cried to the

Giver of All Life to touch the hearts of All His Relations, to find the love hidden in their souls.

Tzegojuñí awoke in a darkened cavern with his uncle, Child of Water, leaning over him. After a time he asked his uncle if he was in the Place of Souls, but Child of Water shook his head and told him to rest quietly. Tzegojuñí had been there five sleeps. They had taken him and were in the process of healing him. Tzegojuñí did not understand this last part and began to voice his confusion. Then he remembered why he was there. He cried tears of joy, for he knew he was successful in his quest. He began to speak to his uncle again, but again Child of Water told him to rest. Then his uncle got up and left the cavern.

Tzegojuñí laid there for what seemed like hours, thinking of his request to the spirits, of his future. He cried and cried, and he asked Changing Mother to give him a little of her strength. His crying and prayers were interrupted by the appearance of his aunt, Tashiña. She carried with her a medicine pouch. Her face was kind and she wore her hair loose. She knelt beside him and kissed his brow. There was a pot of water boiling behind her. She then took his hands and held them close to her heart. He was very sensitive to everything. He drew his hands back and looked at his aunt. She was still of snake blood. But she had changed greatly; she had become the legendary dragon he had heard mentioned in prophecy.

Tashiña made a paste of leaves Tzegojuñí did not know. She sang a healing song and chewed some datura, then blew on his skin. Then she applied the paste and wrapped his body in cloth. Tzegojuñí fell asleep dreaming of his mother.

Tzegojuñí continued to stay with his aunt and uncle, drinking broth and eating the food they brought him. In a few sleeps he awoke in a sweat with a fearful pounding in his head. He began to get cold and his teeth chattered so he thought they would shatter.

He tossed all night in such agony. When his aunt came to see him in the morning he had calmed down a little. But she looked at him and smiled, for the transformation had begun. Tzegojuñí saw and felt the changes of his body, and again he was besieged by fever and chills. His body began to buck with such fury he was powerless to stop it. His aunt hurried out and returned with two men. They had strips of rawhide in their hands. As they tied Tzegojuñí down, Tashiña told them that the restraints would keep him from hurting himself during the final phases of transition. But by now Tzegojuñí was tortured by the highly sensitive sensations that seemed to be consuming his body. Tzegojuñí did not know how long this lasted because he was out of his head. He saw many things during his ordeal; the only peace he knew was when his mother came and smiled at him in the fitful dreams.

Then one day he returned to his body. He was awakened by Grandfather Sun's warmth as it lit up the cave walls. Tzegojuñí smelled broth and got a little hungry. He pulled himself up and looked at his body. It was covered with a pale salve. Many changes had taken place. It was there on that day, while he looked at his new form, that Tzegojuñí knew the prophecies would be fulfilled; the magic did indeed exist upon the land.

From that day forward a new medicine power was known and honored because of Tzegojuñí's transformation. Tzegojuñí was no longer a he, but a she—the first *nadlé,* "one who is transformed," a two-soul. She was a recognized part of the natural order of the universe. For the healing of the world a balance of male and female energies was necessary; the nadlé provided this, just as it was instituted that there should be Holy Ones.

Becoming a Sacred One involved Tzegojuñí taking on various roles and responsibilities. She was summoned to councils, and nothing was decided for many years without first seeking her advice.

Finally, through her path of leading an extraordinary life, she crossed to the Realm of Spirit. She and the power of the nadlé were considered so powerful a transmuting force that their mere presence could turn ambition into inspiration.

Tzegojuñí in the feminine form became famous for the ability to assess individuals by their accomplishments rather than by their gender. She was also noted for her healing knowledge. She acquired a widespread reputation as having supernatural powers and the gift of prophecy. Even the animal clans recognized this power and respected it.

Intimates through Time

Apachería. At first glance, the territory appears to be a barren, inhospitable wasteland with no redeeming features. For countless miles, the desert stretches away in seemingly endless waves of shimmering deep-cut arroyos, appearing to be populated by little more than snakes, cacti, and an occasional wild chicory. When Lynda and I arrived in August 1996, the sun commanded the vast blue sky, shining mercilessly over the desolate landscape of Salt River Canyon, crushing human and beast alike beneath a heavy blanket of heat.

And yet it isn't all like this. There is water, if you know where to look, and food. There are breathtaking sunsets and glorious dawns. And beyond the arid flats there are hidden canyons sheltered between high cliff sentinels, secret places where legends and prophecies were born.

There cool water and sweet grass are abundant, and game is plentiful. Deer, rabbits, bear, squirrels, and wild turkeys can all be found within the high protective walls.

I had returned on sacred pilgrimage to heal my soul sickness. As I looked out, nothing moved on the face of the land, yet I knew my ancestors were out there waiting. I could feel their eyes on me and sense their anticipation as they watched my return home.

There was a surprising change in the scenery as we got closer to my family's canyon. Cottonwood and cedar grew closer together. I imagined a shrill cry echoing off the rock walls as we entered. Lights exploded behind my eyes and the sounds of the present receded into the distance as a haze of gray mist settled around me.

At that moment I was at the Doorway of the Snake. A fountain of water burst from a rock wall, providing a continual rainbow with clear water flowing near the cave entrance. Nestled within the natural baffle of mesas and mountains, this holy place has been seen by few outsiders.

I wandered into the surrounding area to collect wood for our evening fire. As I reached a higher vantage point, I could see our camp beneath me, protected by the high canyon walls, hidden from the outside world. I carried the firewood to the pit and built a fire, concentrating on the legend of Tzegojuñí and how it currently applied to our lives.

Lynda and I had chosen to be life mates; we are partners of the same gender. We are familiar with all the prejudices. Many like us cry out against this injustice. As long as there is prejudice humans will never be able to fairly know one another.

And, yes, it is prejudice that keeps us from knowing ourselves. Think about it: As long as there are walls that separate we cannot have the connection to Spirit. As long as we do not see ourselves as One with All then we shall never have the fortitude for a spiritual quest. As long as we adhere to prejudices there can never be a genuine perception of unconditional love. This applies to all prejudices, not just those against the nadlé, or two-soul, as my tradition calls this phenomena.

As Lynda approached, kneeled, and touched her lips to my cheek, I thought to myself, *No mother thinks her child ugly, because her child is her creation. In the same way we create ourselves. To reach any sort of spiritual realization, prejudices must be confronted and resolved.*

Everything seemed frozen in time there. A shiver touched me as a chipmunk sounded an alarm. Visual energy shifts increased with a crow's haunting caw. The animals carry no such intellectual maladies.

Staring into the sky I remembered the blazing constellation that swirled above us the night before, and with Lynda I was allowed to fly with them. I saw worlds beyond time. I knew the source of this ability; the Mountain Spirits had blessed us according to the sacredness of our lives.

Tzegojuñí's was a very, very old story that was told in the dead of winter, late at night, when Grandfather Owl hooted across the frozen grasses. Like all stories I learned as a child, it carried a lesson and a truth. Some say it was born of the wind and nurtured of the soul. The words filled my memory, mingled with thoughts of my own. In the distance, Grandmother Crow cawed and chuckled.

In childhood I had learned of this place; the ghosts of my ancestors gathered here. I could trace my heritage back to the original Snake Children and claim kinship. This legend held a puzzle; it contained sacredness. I had been called to this canyon. In the firelight I looked away, seeing into the past—into the Doorway of the Snake.

I sensed a presence. Goosepimples appeared on my neck as if unseen eyes were watching. The presence seemed to pulse, study, gauge.

I was taught how to see. An odd angle, a shade of color, or a break in the uneven latticework might be the only clue available. But I could find nothing out of place. The sensation had been part of the dream.

I shook myself free of a shiver. But I also knew that dreams were real in the make-believe world of the Tlish Diyan, as real as something you can touch. The sensation of the dream had jolted me. A thrill, tingling with the intensity and pleasure of ecstasy, had bolted along my nerves, reaching the depths of my soul.

The cawing of the crow sounded louder.

In the darkness of the night, sudden warmth bathed over me. I forced myself to move. The air seemed to sparkle in crystalline form around me.

"You've come," said a voice that sounded strong, vital.

"Tzego?"

As my vision adjusted, I located Tzegojuñí's form where he stood near the cliff wall. Power radiated from the being like heat from a glowing hot rock. Tzegojuñí eyed me. "Naylin 'iskiñihí," he began, "don't be inhibited. If you hold back from achieving your heart's desire you will become bitter and frustrated. If you hold back from expressing yourself your creativity will stagnate. If you hold back from taking action you will become impotent with timidity. Don't stop anything. Let your uniqueness flow freely."

"Yes." I gave a kind smile. "I know."

"In the beginning, you had to adhere to structure until you attained that proper understanding of how to behave with uninhibited spontaneity. If you had attempted to be uninhibited without actually being uninhibited, then you would have looked like a class clown. Thus you spent a certain amount of time studying structure until there was no longer a need for structure. Now you have thoroughly absorbed the secret of moderation and you are able to act with responsibility and spontaneity. True uninhibitedness has come as a by-product of your sure, fresh, and creative actions."

I wet my lips nervously, as if after all these years hearing and seeing visions was an unusual event. "Thank you," I answered "I will walk my path honoring my innate dignity and actualizing my inborn abilities, for I have come to understand that this is the path to authentic power."

"You, who have known ignorance, bigotry, and injustice," the being whispered into my ear, "are a shining example of unconditional love and pure intent. You endeavor to understand and forgive. Claim the purity of your sacred self and let it shine radiantly for all to see and share in its warmth. Personify the qualities of understanding, perception, and sacred wisdom. Your time is Now." The words made my heart pound.

"Yes, Uncle," I answered in a small voice. Two tears left my eyes, tracing fine lines through the dust on my face.

The story of Tzegojuñí's transformation and the balancing of the male-female energies was told and retold wherever the two-leggeds sat around their campfires. To this day a traditional circle that counts a nadlé among its members is considered very fortunate. The success of the transition into the Fifth World of Peace and Ilumination is believed to be assured. This respect is apparent in all aspects, as nadlé medicine brings joy and goodness to all.

A nadlé is to be respected. They are the bridges between male and female, human and Spirit. They are, somehow, sacred and holy.

And so it is.

10
Cahokia and the Festival of Joy

In the past the legend of "Cahokia and the Festival of Joy" was part of a living tradition. But today the knowledge of manifesting dreams and the tradition of oral teachings have dimmed. Defeat clouds the vision of most people. Discovering the power of our Earth-Spirit connection means fulfilling the divine purpose of self-actualization. Changing Mother below calls in unprecedented ways. To find the Path of Healing we must walk with the same determination and integrity as the Ancients.

The Legend

Long ago two of the people, a father and son, lived in the village above the Doorway of the Snake. In those faraway days the son, Blue Dawn, was learning the great medicine powers of his clan. Pouches of healing herbs hung from the rafters of the family's wickiup.

Besides learning the medicine ways, Blue Dawn was young and tall, strong and handsome. All the girls of the village thought it was a shame that he had not taken a wife. For him the shyest dimples erupted and the broadest smiles flashed, but he took no notice. Many gifts found their way to his home, but Blue Dawn paid no more attention to the gifts than to their benefactors. He simply continued his studies; all would be revealed in time.

Two of Blue Dawn's admirers were sisters. Both were very pretty and young, but they used their medicine powers for selfish goals instead of for benefiting the whole. When all the other girls gave up, discouraged at Blue Dawn's lack of interest, the sisters kept coming day after day, trying to win his favor. At last the attention became so annoying to Blue Dawn that he could not sleep. Two nights had passed sleeplessly, until he felt as though he would climb right out of his skin.

On the third night he finally gave up. The night was strange and he was feeling pensive. At last he decided to hire a village crier to go through the circle of wickiups and announce that in four days' time he would choose a wife. The announcement of his impending choice caused a great scampering of feet. The girls ran out of the wickiups to catch every word; when the crier had passed by they ran back into their homes to prepare themselves for the competition. The two sisters worked hardest of all; day and night for four days they applied all the magic they knew.

To Blue Dawn the dream he held seemed so close. He was afraid the rushing of time might chase it away. He dropped his head in his hands and closed his eyes. A background of stars blazed to life on the fabric of his soul. Glorious! Too many stars to count. Stars like frost crystals spread endlessly across a grassy meadow on a cold morning. They gleamed and twinkled at Blue Dawn.

When Blue Dawn told his father and the Elders about his plan they were silent. "I go in search of my wife. I am going to the Place of Souls. I believe she is there." Efforts from his father and the others to dissuade him did no good. He set out on his way.

Blue Dawn watched the hawks a lot as he traveled, hoping they would speak and give him answers. It was mating season. He watched them whirl and dive and grab at each other with their feet as they tumbled in the air. Of the two red-tails the female was larger. She hadn't made up her mind about the male. First they came close. Then they hovered right out in front over the canyon rim he followed. The air rose in the warmth of the day. They liked the rising air; it made it easier for them to float.

After Blue Dawn had traveled for several days, Old Man Thunder appeared to the young man. He asked, "Where are you going?"

"I am going to the Place of Souls to look for a wife."

"Even if you travel until you grow old you will never get there in time to take a wife," Old Man Thunder replied. "The Place of Souls is too far for you to reach. Go no further in this quest; seek a wife among those of your village." After saying this, Old Man Thunder turned himself into his spirit form and then back into a man again. The youth was frightened and impressed, but he could not let the chief of the Thunder Beings deter him. He insisted on continuing his journey.

After the young man had traveled further, Gentle Deer, chief of the Deer Clan, appeared, also in human form. Again Blue Dawn was admonished to go back. Despite the second warning, he insisted on continuing. "The Doorway of the Snake is closer than the Place of Souls, and that is as far as you can go," said Gentle Deer. "After visiting the Doorway, you must return to your own people." Reluctantly, Blue Dawn agreed to this.

After the youth had gone another short distance, Itzá, the eagle, appeared. He warned Blue Dawn again, "You can only go to the

Doorway of the Snake; no further. The snakes may try to bite you if you display any fear. Use this herb to see past that illusion. In the middle of the Doorway lives the leader of the Snake Clan, Nakía, and you should see him right away. This clan is made up of shapeshifters, who can change themselves into two-leggeds at will."

When Blue Dawn reached the Doorway of the Snake the snakes did indeed test him, but he ate the herb, his fear dissipated, and they retreated. He reached Nakía unharmed and was received kindly, though Nakía also warned Blue Dawn not to proceed any further.

Now, in those days Cahokía, daughter of Kato'ya and Kaliña and sister of Nakía, had not yet taken a mate. She was a very beautiful girl. As Blue Dawn talked with Nakía, he glanced deeper into the cavern. Two snakes danced the dance of love; it was the season. Cahokía was moving her body back and forth in rhythmic support. Blue Dawn could just see her silhouette. As he watched her body arch back and forth, he forgot about his talk with the snake leader.

"She's getting to be a real woman," said Nakía. "It's a pity that one so young and handsome would search for a mate among those in the Place of Souls. Cahokía's winters ride well on her."

Blue Dawn continued to watch.

"Yes, she is a woman of marrying age," continued Nakía. "I suppose one of the fine young men of the village will see that she gets everything she needs."

Blue Dawn looked at Nakía, but the man was looking into the distance, out of the cavern, watching a pair of white-headed eagles circling in the blue sky.

By this time, back in the village a long line of girls were coming to see Blue Dawn's father. The fourth day would arrive with the passing of the night and Blue Dawn had yet to return. There was quite a bit of commotion over this.

In the Doorway of the Snake, Blue Dawn quickly rose from

where he sat and took Cahokía by the hand, saying, "You are the one who shall be my wife. You shall never want for anything."

He sighed heavily as he drank in the beauty of the night and of his bride. Life was good. He loved Cahokía. He loved her as he never thought to love any woman! She had touched his heart and melted his soul. He never knew it could be so. That night Blue Dawn promised Cahokía that her life would be a great adventure and that the two of them would be together always.

The next morning Blue Dawn awoke to ancient chants. He ran his fingers over Cahokía and hugged her gently as she slept before moving to prepare for their journey home. When Cahokía and Blue Dawn arrived back at the two-legged village, the two sisters saw it all. Slipping away, they vowed vengeance on Cahokía.

Blue Dawn and his sweet wife were happy together. It was not long before she announced that they would soon welcome a little one to their home. Now more than ever Blue Dawn said to her, "Cahokía, beware of the sisters; the storm of evil rages in the lakes of their minds. May the magic of your medicine stop the gales of unnecessary assault, and in your womb hold the reflection of our child's soul, protected in the light of our love."

Cahokía just smiled for a moment and then said, "Husband, you must release your fear. I will dive deep for the pearls of wisdom. I am strong of conscience, and fear will never destroy me. If I cannot discover a solution of compassion I will not give up. I will be aware of my approach. I will seek friendship again and again, always diving deeper for introspective healing in all situations, until I embrace you as an immortal and shower our child with the sacred rain of joy and our love."

One day, close to Cahokía's birthing time, the sisters came to the wickiup and said, "Blue Dawn, we go to gather the agavé. Will you not let your wife go with us?"

The sisters had attempted nothing in the months that Cahokía had lived in the village, so Blue Dawn replied, "Oh, yes, she may go." But taking his wife aside he again said, "Now be sure that while you are with them you take heed."

Cahokía promised and started away with the sisters. As she walked with the other two women, she played the events of her life over and over in her head until it began to take on a dreamlike essence. She was married to a wise and generous man and would soon give birth to their first child. Was this real or just a dream—the kind of fanciful creation of an imaginative soul? Was she really here?

Suddenly, white lightening flashed across the torn and rugged clouds. Storms came on fast in this area. The first drops of rain splattered down and then the fury of the storm broke loose above the women. The wind gusted ferociously out of the sky, slicing through the upper branches of pine. The land shivered and swayed around the three women. Eventually the storm overwhelmed them all.

As the storm approached, filling the world with darkness, Blue Dawn began to search the horizon. When faint lavender light finally drained the gray from the world, it was easier to see. Blue Dawn walked to the wickiup of the sisters with long, quick strides.

"Sisters," he asked them very sternly. "Where is my wife?"

"Why, isn't she at home?" asked the deceitful sisters, as if greatly surprised. "She began to feel the pains and left to return home long before we did."

High above, a streak of life burned greenish as a star fell across the clearing sky.

Taking one last look at the sisters, Blue Dawn turned on his heel and walked away.

From the time Cahokía disappeared all went wrong at the village, for Blue Dawn held the well-being of all his people, even unto life and death. Blue Dawn had been hurt badly. He was suddenly unsure of himself and his people. Only someone very wicked would harm an important woman like Cahokía and her unborn child. The two that had tricked her would be hounded by the power of her clan for the rest of their days. He was sure of this, for Cahokía was one of Creation's own, a supernatural.

The events provoked unprecedented turbulence in Blue Dawn's emotions. As time passed, increasingly abnormal events and correspondingly high levels of stress arose to shake the grieving husband's faith.

The wise ones of the village became frustrated trying to reach the man's spirit before it became so fragmented that it was beyond recovery. They watched him and wondered what Blue Dawn saw in the roots of his soul. Had the loss destroyed him? Would he fight to hold on? How would he accept the devastation that possessed him? Would he release his dream, and then let it eat at his soul the way cactus acid ate through shell? Or would he reach through the fire of his pain, knowing that the heart would sear, and then heal?

The temperature had dropped slightly and the thin sliver of the moon wore a faint halo, indicating moisture in the air. Before that the blood-red sun had hung over the irregular horizon, streaming through the wickiup doors. It was decided that there must be another effort made to find Cahokía. Blue Dawn had searched in vain and the people had helped him, but perhaps another perspective was needed.

They took the sacred tobacco, *na-toh,* rolled in cornhusk to Itzá, the eagle, whose eyes were sharpest of all the Holy Parents' children. Giving him their sacred prayers, they said, "Grandfather Itzá, the consciousness of the people is small. It lays barren of life force since Cahokía has gone. We exist in the land of the dead and have fallen prey to scarcity. Please help us."

Itzá accepted the two-leggeds' prayers, flying upward into the sky. Higher and higher he rose, in great circles, while his eyes peered through the shadows, witnessing Blue Dawn's fear—a spirit gone wrong.

At last he came back and softly said, "It is not for me to find Cahokía. The Giver of All Life has shown me that we are an extended family of spiritual origin. Reap ways to manifest your whispered prayers from the field of plenty."

Then the people went with an offering to Coyote and begged him to find his relation. Coyote started off with his nose to the ground, trying to find his niece. He trotted all over as the rain of desire fell many times, and yet he did not find his relation.

Then the troubled people got Badger to search, for he was aggressive and they knew he would never give up. Badger returned advising, "To find Cahokía you must first learn to use the gift of the Holy Parents' love in your hearts, to love the whole more than yourselves. You must love your community more than your family. Expand, so that you may love outsiders more than your community, and you must love your world and All Your Relations more than any one individual or self."

The people felt very sad and were deaf to the messages they received. They traveled to Osprey, whose healing insights could be seen beyond all illusion and disease. But he too returned with the challenge of higher spirit. "You must learn to love the sacredness of Changing Mother more than anything else, for it is her love with which you embrace everything. Without Changing Mother, you cannot love anyone or anything."

By this time ripples and changes had come to the world. Power ebbed and flowed. The animal clans knew that no matter how one might start his or her healing path of evolution, he or she couldn't always be counted on to follow through. As the two-leggeds went on searching in their illusion of defeat the animals prayed, "Changing Mother, teach our younger siblings to love the whole and serve the whole. Teach them to be true to their words, even as they want others to be true to them. Teach them to love others as they wish us to love them. Teach them, Sacred Mother, to make others happy, to make others smile. Teach them, Changing Mother, to find their happiness in the joy of others. May our siblings be strong, and unto the seventh generation bring honor and abundance to the great Circle of Life, to those that have gone on before, and to All Our Relations."

The people were at a loss. Their fields dwindled, water was scarce. At last they thought they would go to Owl, the guardian of the dead, for surely Cahokía was dead or they would have found her by now.

So they went to Grandfather Owl and pleaded with him. Owl wept when he saw Blue Dawn, and said, "Truly I will look. I will take the sun and put it in my heart. I will take the moon and pull it to my belly. I will draw down the Star Path and merge with the northern star as the golden dawn disk edges the purple cliffs. Before now, how many of you understood Cahokía's purpose in your lives?" And he spread his wings and climbed up into the sky.

When he got back the people all asked, "Did you see nothing?"

"Oh, I saw many things," Grandfather Owl said. "I saw that everything is temporary. Nothing remains the same. Of all the mysteries I witnessed, the most perplexing was why the two-leggeds do not embrace their own power.

"Generation after generation of accumulated knowledge has been offered to you. It will continue. There are days coming where your vision will be clear and your thoughts as sharp as fractured obsidian. Dance the Dance of Life. Cahokía has shattered her mortal flame in the Dance of Illumination to show, smilingly, that her spirit remains strong.

"With devotion she has broken the hard encrusted cover of delusion that coated her. She embraced the Dance of Life and, forever and ever, has released all her desires, weaknesses, and mortality, and joined with the Dance of Eternity. Now you, my family, must dance in celebration of life and love to find your beloved Cahokía."

"Oh!" cried Blue Dawn, speaking for the first time. "Go, my friend, and gather a bouquet of variously hued flowers of love."

Off flew Owl, and in a few minutes he returned holding out the tender, fragrant, blooming branches. From this orchestra of fragrances the bee of community service made its way to the silence of the village's heart. Blue Dawn accepted this flower garden of the heart, and in honor of the sweet fragrance of his love's breath he walked silently and solemnly to his wickiup while all the wondering people followed in the dew of sweetness released from the heart of the flowers.

When Blue Dawn came inside his wickiup once more he took a new blanket and spread it in the middle of the floor. He laid the flowers at the altar of his heart, in tribute to All That Is. Covering them with another blanket, he realized that the rarest love grew in the garden of his sacred space and now lay before him. Would the Sacred Power receive this offering?

Dressing himself in the splendid buckskins that his wife had made him and taking his rattle in his right hand, he seated himself at the head of the blanket and sang, "Eternal Flame, shoot little spirit arrows into each human consciousness. Connect their flames to All That Is. You are the many-divided flames of living souls spreading through eternity. But you are one, the Eternal Flame, when our souls join in unconditional love."

When he had finished the song all could see that the flowers had begun to grow, lifting the blanket a little. Blue Dawn shook his gourd, and still the flowers kept growing. Again and again he sang.

When he had finished a fourth time it was plain to all that a human form lay between the two blankets. And when he sang his song the fifth time, the form sat up and moved. Tenderly he lifted away the upper blanket and there sat his sweet snake wife, finer than ever, alive, and holding their first child!

For four days the people danced and sang in *Hedo-wa-chee,* the Festival of Joy. Blue Dawn was happy again, and now the rain began to fall. Changing Mother drank, was glad, and was green, and the crops came to life.

When Cahokía told Blue Dawn that the sisters had watched her get swept away by a flash flood, he was very angry. But Cahokía explained that all this was a necessary part of her growing, and even he had played an instrumental part in the Rite of Passage with his fearful obsessing. She suggested he pray to release his feelings, and he did: "Giver of All Life, save me from attacks of fear, which burn my brain, shock my nerves, and poison my blood.

"Giver of All Life, when I am afraid, place me before a great smoking mirror of reflection, where I may see my face full of terror and rage. Giver of All Life, I do not like to be seen this way, so do not let me make my appearance before others with such a darkened shadow.

"Changing Mother, show me how to release this emotion that rattles the foundations of my life, which makes me and others so unhappy and miserable. Bless me and my family, that I may never spoil the love of those I hold dear.

"Bless me, that I will not feed my fear by allowing myself to become still more terrorized. Cure my fear with respect and kindness. Command my kindness to remain as undisturbed as a lake in the time of Two Lights.

"Giver of All Life, help me to always recognize that one who tries to harm others is an injured being who deserves my compassion, not my reproach. All are my relatives; may I love them as you love me."

Cahokía pulled her medicine pouch from her neck, feeling its familiarity. The people had gathered to hear her words, so she chose them carefully.

"I have soared high above the illusion of pettiness to which human nature clings. I have soared higher and higher. I flew above the clouds. My mind became free of the ignorance that used to attack my inner peace. I flew with balanced energies, above the tornadoes of worry. I flew higher and higher, and I climbed to the Sacred Lodge of our most Holy Parents. I saw my father, Kato'ya, and my mother, Kaliña.

"I was shown that we must celebrate our oneness with the sacred Changing Mother. Our songs must boom on the shores of the consciousness of everyone we reach out to in our daily lives. We must break the limiting burdens we have created for ourselves. May our Hedo-wa-chee rattle through bodies, minds, souls, surroundings, villages, Changing Mother, the Cloud Nations—All That Is. Let us unite our intent with our prayers, that we might do the work we have been put upon Earth to do."

Hedo-wa-chee, the Festival of Joy

The morning was cold and a light rain trickled off the house. Beneath the rolling clouds the mesa looked as green as the waters of the creek, and the first flowers had opened. I led Little Wolf, my dog, from the house toward the grove where we liked to take our morning walk. I didn't notice that my hiking boots were soaked through or that the cloud haze hung heavy and low over the mountain. Nor did I notice the presence that approached from the rock outcropping above the sacred Stone People Lodge, until I felt the dog tug back against the lead. I lifted my head and saw the Coyote, and then I stopped.

Libaye didn't waste any words. "I am giving you a special gift," he said. "I will let you see through my eyes." And so Libaye and I spoke of the legend of Hedo-wa-chee, the Festival of Joy, and how these celebrations came into existence.

"Hedo-wa-chee is a time of feasting and demonstrating gratitude. Rituals are performed that ensure a good year and align the magnetics of humanity with those of the Changing Mother . . . ." The words trailed off and hung in the wet, thick air.

Libaye looked down toward the creek. It had begun to run higher in the last few nights from the early spring rains. Soon it would be off-color, rushing, rolling brush in its course through the bed. "During the days of ceremony," he said, "clan business is conducted. Hours are spent in serious council. Internal matters are dealt with: disputes settled, dreams negotiated, and in many cases, counting coup sung."

"We seek order, and we find only truth. In winter, all things appear dead or dormant. The rain and cold seem incessant, the nights long. Then the day comes and the sky clears to a brilliant blue. The air warms. A mist rises from the earth and the perfume of water, clay, and moss drifts through the air. You prepare the spring equinox Ceremony of the Hawk. The people are optimistic; they know that there is an end to the cold.

"Far too often, they see the responsibilities of our path as time-consuming irritants. They see the activities as obligations, and they strain against their time in the silence. But I know there to be a joy in working in harmony with the proper time and energy. When we do things in the flow of the energy, those efforts bear the fruit of healing, and the gratification is tremendous.

"That is the optimism born of Cahokía's tale. That is the inno-cence and the belief of the child within."

Grandfather Sun's face shimmered silver-white through the film of clouds that rode out of the northwest. His light was just barely bright enough to penetrate the shimmering veil. Pale white light bathed the land, illuminating the sacred site.

My life was altered by the venom of the Snake Clan when I was quite young. On this day I knew the extent of the power of Cahokía and the Hedo-wa-chee deep within my soul.

Libaye stood on the ridge above Little Wolf and I. As he sighed his shoulders lowered and he said, "How many times have you led Hedo-wa-chee? This time of celebrating the Spirit and embracing the power of love with others is wondrous. Cahokía awaits you even now. Anticipation shines forth from her eyes."

Libaye stepped forward slightly and sniffed the air.

"Cahokía knows the frustration you are feeling about getting people to listen and take life celebration seriously. You inherited a bit of her soul. So alike, so different. But then, the Giver of All Life determined that long ago. Perhaps that faraway time, many life-times past, led to this moment. We can't know the workings of All That Is; they just go on around us, presenting us with lessons and opportunities daily."

As I watched Libaye walk back up the hill I felt both lighter and sadder.

Three days later I stood on the vista overlooking the house. It was a beautiful little place. We were truly blessed to be able to live here a while.

An arrow's arc to the northwest lay the Viejas Ranchero and Casino. In the late morning sun the buildings looked as pale as doe-skin. Many went there to wager their dreams on the pull of a slot bandit's arm or the turn of a card. I had been to the casino once and it reminded me of chaos in action. It made me smile to think of all the good things the money from the enterprise did for the tribe, however. But I choose not to be part of it.

I had come to this area to celebrate the spring equinox Hedo-wa-chee, Hawk's Living Your Vision Celebration. Winter is passing into Spring. Summer is on the other side. Celebrating life is Hedo-wa-chee; when we first experience the energy it is magical. Then we raise the vibration and heal. On the other side is a new vista of perception. Celebrating the cycles of connecting love we emerge like a dragon, soaring in the sky.

I had not told my aunty and uncle, but it appeared there would only be four of us celebrating the powerful energy this year. Perhaps we could incorporate the spirit of San Diego's annual powwow to increase the vibration a tad more. A powwow is a good place to go and laugh and be with family.

It will be a good day, I thought as I looked down at the house. Uncle and I would dance in honor of our ancestors. The idea didn't exactly displease me, but I was sad that more people didn't take these celebrations seriously. In the days of my great-great-grandparents the celebrations would draw people from the Four Directions. There would be hundreds in attendance for the purifying, dancing, and feasting—so many people that the celebration would run for four days. Now so few came that I was reduced to planning all the momentous steps in one day. In spite of the sadness I felt, I smiled. *At least Lynda and I still remember,* I thought, *and we honor the vibrations of Changing Mother.*

As I walked down the hill to the house, I thought of the vow I had made to my grandfather, the vow that the legends and traditions would live on through our family. I now had two granddaughters, and one would someday carry the bundle of our clan and the other the vessel of balanced power so that the vow would be fulfilled.

I stopped for a moment in the garden and lifted my hands as if to touch the sky. I remembered the legend of Cahokía as grandfather had told of the origin of the Hedo-wa-chee. I had been young then and it all had seemed so simple. There were only the people, the firelight, and the coyotes howling in the distance. Now my grandfather was dead and his responsibilities had been passed to my shoulders. It would be better to celebrate the spring equinox at the powwow than to be alone and focused on that solitary energy.

I looked up at my hands. Many winters ago my grandfather had said that if you went to sleep with your palms out the stars would come down and rest in them and you would be a powerful person. Many nights I remembered waking up with my arms straight up in the air, numb, not quite sure how they had gotten there or what was holding them up. I lowered my arms and went into the house.

Three nights later Nakía came to me at about ten o'clock in the evening. I had gone to bed but I was not asleep. He came into our room and stood close to me. He sat down beside me and touched my face, nose, and lips.

He said, "You are coming into your own power and with that comes adventure. Naylin 'iskiñihí, all your life you have sought peace and the search has led you into many wrong directions. You must look into peace and find its beating heart. I am going to help you. You will go to sleep, but when you awake the patterned illusions will begin to slip away and the energy of reality will begin to become clear. You've seen this on occasion, but as the illusion fades the clarity of reality will stay for longer periods of time. You will see as I see—into both dimensions. Open your eyes, Naylin 'iskiñihí. Do it now. See the transition!" I did not speak a word. He stood up, walked to the window, and went away.

According to Nakía the practical side of our nature can wrap itself around our confusion when it swells and slowly squeeze it toward understanding. Life is reordered through ceremony. Seeing through two perceptions puts our soul back in harmony with All That Is.

Hedo-wa-chee is a living and valid tradition of life celebration, comparable to a river with a long course. It brings freshness, richness, and abundance. There is support for our endeavors. The importance of Hedo-wa-chee in contemporary times is the same as in times long gone: Participants come together to combine their energies to manifest the greatness of their love in the physical world. We carry the knowledge, and through the dance we find our way to healing. The songs, prayers, and legends are beautiful words. We live the esoteric spiritual principles of the Ancestors— changing time, timeless life values—and today we are able to manifest the power of that spirit through our stories and celebrations.

Mokesh Battles
the Aztecs

"Mokesh Battles the Aztecs" was an essential story during the beginning of my spiritual path. I am devoted to the wisdom that the story embodies. Spirit is the creation of ideology. The true experience is living in my own life. My life is sacred.

Through Mokesh I learned the true meaning of what it meant to be a warrior. For my ancestors, the ability to have the courage to know self and confront fear were the attributes of a truly honorable warrior. The task is to awaken to the possibilities that affirm life. To look beyond the energy of a situation and see the opportunities for resolution, healing, growth, and peace. This is what the evolution of humanity is really all about.

The Legend

A line of men trading blocks of salt approached the canyon that surrounded the village. The men were from a nearby area, and the salt, which they obtained by evaporating salt spring water, was priceless here. Within the village women and men eagerly awaited the traders. But the traders had to be patient, for no one entered the mountain hideaway until his identity had been properly announced by the callers standing on the precipices of the cliff walls.

While passing single-file through the narrow entrance to the cool canyon floor, the traders almost collided with some outgoing hunters. As soon as the traders passed the hunters, the villages gave way to the frenzy of barter. This village was distinctly known for its finely crafted obsidian blades and leatherwork. The traders laid down their burdens while their leader engaged in lively bargaining with the villagers.

All the activity in the village did not go unobserved, for atop the great Spirit Cliff stood the village's famed leader, Chu'hongva (Tattooed Snake), who occasionally peered down on the scene below. But it was not the bartering in the village that concerned this man of integrity. Rather it was the doings within a circle of evenly spaced stones just on the other side of the village that commanded his attention. His uncle, Mokesh, was sitting on a stone positioned at the center of the ring. The seated man peered at the sun and then at the shadows cast by the stones. Over and over again his eyes moved from the sky to the ground, and from time to time he would speak to his invisible guide. He was making solar calculations, for he was the Keeper of Time, and from that circle he calculated propitious moments for activities such as planting, harvesting, and the commencement of religious celebrations. On this day Mokesh, youngest son of Kato'ya and Kaliña, was seeking solar signs that the time was right to begin a ritual initiation to pass his power to an apprentice.

Normally an apprentice began training for the role early in life. Under the tutelage of the grandparent, uncle, or aunt, the medicine power of the Elder would be passed. But Mokesh had no children, no one with whom to share his knowledge. Tattooed Snake had tried but was unable to grasp the concepts that had been put before him. Now he felt sorrow for his ancient uncle.

Of the many celebrations the people observed in their Hedo-wa-chee, or Festival of Joy, the Snake Children's Fire of Healing was one of the most spectacular. The rite, held in late summer during the Moon of Little Changes, was meant to bring the rain that guaranteed a good final harvest. The snake, with its zigzag movements, symbolized lightning, rain, and the return of Tattooed Snake's grandfather, Kato'ya.

The entire ceremony had been conceived by his mother, Cahokía, and was now watched over by his uncle during its sixteen sacred days. For the first few days Mokesh prepared himself by praying, purifying, fashioning prayer feathers, and setting up altars around the canyon. Then each morning for four days Mokesh went into the Doorway of the Snake to commune with his brother the Snake Leader, Nakía. On the eighth day there was the reenactment of Mystic Marriage, a ritualistic joining of Kato'ya and Kaliña, Tattooed Snake's grandparents.

Also on the eighth day the men of the village danced while holding the harvest of the season. The stamping of their feet was used to draw the attention of the Sacred Changing Mother to their celebration in honor of her sacrifice to her children.

On the last day the Snake Clan entered the village. Clan members had the ability to tell if one was of a pure and sincere heart by draping their bodies over the dancers, where they would sleep if the individual exhibited no fear. That climactic day ended at sunset while men raced to align the polar energies and women cheered them on.

Since that ceremony Mokesh had been nearly silent. Tattooed Snake squatted out of sight and watched his uncle in the circle. Then he released the essence of his prayers—voiced upon the ethers of the sacred smoke ritual—and listened to the hum of the village below.

Later Tattooed Snake sat with Mokesh outside the old man's wickiup. They enjoyed the warm sun and talked about the power of the Snake Clan.

Upon returning to his own wickiup Tattooed Snake stirred a pot of soup. As the fire died down he listened to the wail of a coyote. He could barely make it out, and he thought that it had come close to the village in search of food. It cried out again, and the canyon carried its voice to the heavens. Tattooed Snake snuggled down into the blankets next to his wife, Do-kliñi, and listened but did not hear his cousin again, only the breeze as it sang in unison with the cottonwood leaves. He closed his eyes and tried to sleep, but this was a restless time and sleep was not soon in coming.

On the day Mokesh was to name his apprentice, Tattooed Snake heard voices and shouts and he saw children running toward the pass. There was always a lot of commotion in the camp, especially when the traders were in season, and Tattooed Snake suspected it was probably another group in search of a good trade and new stories to tell upon their return home. Out of curiosity he stood and walked in that direction.

By the time he reached the edge of the village, there were already fifteen or twenty people standing there, talking among themselves. "I don't recognize him," said one. "Nor the strange clothes he wears," said another. "He is not from around here," said a third.

The man they spoke of was tall and was dressed in fine cloth and jewelry, with dirt and bruises showing on his body. He walked with a slow, awkward gait, as though he had fallen or walked a great distance with little rest. When the figure was a short distance from the camp he stopped and lowered his head in a submissive pose. Then he continued walking.

Fifty paces from the group the thin man stopped again and shook his head as others stepped forward to help him. Tattooed Snake sucked in his breath. The stranger's face was gaunt, the skin stretched tight over the bones and was ashen in color. The man slid to the ground, fainting, as the people stared on silently.

Tattooed Snake ran to the man, addressing the crowd, "Bring me water, and fetch my Uncle." As he looked at the stranger, Do-kliñi emerged from their wickiup with water. She tried not to cry out as she raised the water to his mouth. The men stared. "What is this? Who could do this to another being?" they asked.

Tattooed Snake turned to the stranger, who had once again lost his battle to the darkness of unconsciousness. The stranger's mouth was open, but no sound had emerged.

The stranger awoke to find several blurred faces surrounding him. A gold eye set in an Ancient's smiling face told him he was safe. "What has happened to you, my friend?"

Silence enveloped the wickiup.

Mokesh stared at the stranger. Yes, the stranger could feel Mokesh's concern over his condition. He felt queasiness in his stomach that had been severe for four days. He tried to straighten up, blinking at Mokesh. "My name is Kokopelli and I am a trader of the Toltec Nation to the south."

The stranger named Kokopelli tensed as a shuffling of feet outside brought news of other strangers on their way to the canyon. They would arrive at dawn.

While Kokopelli lay in Mokesh's wickiup he told the story of how the fire had been drained from his soul. The Toltec people were once a great civilization, but they had been decimated by time and by a barbarian group that was taking over the Southern Hemisphere, the Aztecs. The Aztecs had set ablaze the Toltec cities, and the people were placed in bondage as slaves.

The Aztec battles were highly ritualized. They fought in elaborate plumed headdresses against a din of cacophonous music. Captives became slaves, but most were tortured and killed. Kokopelli was an exception. He was originally from a family of high esteem. The Aztecs had kept him groomed and well fed so that he might later be stripped naked and tortured to death, pleading for mercy before the Aztec god, Quetzalcoatl, the winged serpent.

Mokesh listened intently as Kokopelli continued: "I will tell you how it is with the Aztecs. Their way is bloody and merciless. Their leader once had a tiny power, no greater than the breath of a bird: the power to make words. He is indeed a fanatic and he is inclined toward destruction. There is hatred in his heart for what most sanctify, and love for what is born of his quest for power over others.

"I have dreamed that with my escape his power will be taken away. Someday he will know how he was an arrogant man who applied the poison full strength and poured it from transparent illusion. He does not honor human nature.

"Now Quetzalcoatl comes to blow him away like a small leaf without the strength of the wind. All that will be left for him is to die in silence without a voice because his ignorance made all his noise.

"Friends, this is what I have seen. This is what I believe. He will come for me, for I am the end of his madness."

When Kokopelli gazed around the wickiup, the glow of light from the fire hurt his eyes. The people around him seemed to be alarmed by his tale, trying ineffectively to make him feel welcome and safe. Daggers of pain shot through his body when he tried to move. A queasy sensation possessed him many times that day, so Kokopelli lay curled in the fetal position on a blanket.

Later that afternoon Tattooed Snake tipped his chin to examine the rock outcropping he and Mokesh sat on. "Does he know that the Quetzalcoatl he speaks of is Grandfather? How does the Clan fit into this man's destiny? Can we survive the Aztec rage if they demand to have the stranger returned?"

He waited for an answer until his limited patience ran out. "Uncle?" The energy had gone out of Tattooed Snake's voice and he sat motionless, looking at Mokesh. The canyon was as quiet as death except for the occasional slide of rocks.

Mokesh spoke a prayer to the Giver of All Life and Changing Mother, thanking them for his new apprentice, Kokopelli. Then he said softly to his nephew, "At last I have found the penetrating eyes that contain Space and Heart, Earth and Stars. The power of our clan abounds everywhere.

"Seeking one to pass my power to has yielded endless continuation. The lost vision of the Aztecs, will be found in the pass. Seeking and searching in countless faces, I have found this one.

"I ask Changing Mother to provide me with transmuting heat that I might restore the crystal purity of our people's lives. I shall battle the Aztecs alone and with my internal Eternal Flame. No life of the clan shall be lost."

Tattooed Snake respected Mokesh. The Snake Medicine was one of the most powerful, and Mokesh had been the village's connection. Now his uncle proposed to do single combat with a force of over fifty.

Before they left their spot of high council Tattooed Snake renewed his vow to his clan: "In my prayers I hold Kato'ya's starlit body, adorned with the dark twinkling light of dawn and the gray twilight. I honor my grandfather's return in my uncle, Mokesh, adorned with the Star Path, dressed in rainbows, sporting diamonds of glittering places. I honor your advice, your bravery, and the continuance of our tradition."

Tattooed Snake had known Mokesh all his life and thought he knew the direction of the old man's mind, but this time, as in many others, Mokesh had managed to catch him off balance.

Mokesh began the painful task of standing up. "Let the Aztecs speak," he said simply.

"I refuse to return Kokopelli to them," said Tattooed Snake, helping the old man to his feet.

"Yes, but let us hear their demands and see the eyes of their leader."

In spite of his concern for his uncle's decision that night, Tattooed Snake had to smile at his old uncle's way of being guardian to the people. That was the way Kato'ya had promised.

Mokesh was restless as he chewed a dry stick of meat and watched the Aztec leader gather his forces before Tattooed Snake. The warriors moved in the northern direction of the circle, their dance a slow deliberate fury. It was almost dusk, and he looked back down the canyon floor toward the gateway. The sentinels were in their places high up in the cliff walls, undetected.

Mokesh raised his eyes to the west and followed the canyon rim from south to north until he could pick out the Doorway of the Snake. It barely stood out anymore; trees and brush now hid the entrance and the power of the place was subdued but ever ready. Today it was more than a home and power place to Mokesh, for it was within the Doorway of the Snake that the women and children of this village had been hidden, protected by the clan guardians. Within that cavern, Nakía, his brother, had dreamed the vision of the future and prayed for strength of spirit.

Again he looked to the north. The angry Aztec leader presented his demand to Tattooed Snake. Mokesh was not paying particular attention to the words being said; he was more interested in the body movements and the colors he saw arising from individuals within the Aztec contingency. Such information was valuable when entering the battlefield. He pictured over and over in his mind the desired victorious outcome. Kokopelli had been sent to Mokesh so the ways might be kept alive. He would take Tattooed Snake's daughter, Toho'ma, as a wife. The child they would bear was the next turn of the Wheel of Understanding.

Mokesh smiled to himself—and so it would be. He smiled to think of the faces of the next generations of bundle caretakers, dreaming the course of evolution. And then he thought of his nephew, Tattooed Snake, and the way he was looking at the Aztec leader. That morning Mokesh had counseled him. He felt the fear, anger, and anguish in the leader, so Mokesh came here to pray. He would miss his nephew and the family he had come to call his own. Most of the villagers were a little afraid of him, primarily because of his golden-hued eyes. They were more like what one would find in a wolf than in a man or snake. He told the people that they reflected the harvest of Changing Mother's love. He spent his time tending to the sick and the broken, but even so they did not quite trust him as one of their own.

Mokesh watched as the Aztecs left in an animated display of ferocity. Then Tattooed Snake stood as others quickly gathered around him. The time was near. Mokesh felt his nephew's eyes searching for him. He headed for the village leader. This would be their last night together and there was much to share. He glanced up to the darkening sky and asked his father, Kato'ya, to light his way. From somewhere far off he heard the hoot of Grandfather Owl.

The next morning at sunrise Mokesh squatted near a small spring and mixed yellow pigment into a paste. Then he stood and stripped off his shirt. He dipped his finger into the paint and traced

two lightning streaks from his clavicles to his waist, just as Nakía
had instructed. Then he drew two yellow snakes on each side of his
face, from temple to chin. He said the prayers Nakía had given him
to the directional energies contained within the Wheel of Evolution. He prayed to Old Man Thunder, whose long rumbling voice
foretold the beginning of life and abundance among the many gifts
of Changing Mother.

He prayed to the Giver of All Life, who watched over all things
of the world. He turned his substance over to the Sacred Mother.
Finally he sang his song: "The time is at hand. Refreshed and sanc-
tified, with purpose revealed, I pass through the Gateway of Time
into the Realm of Now, dimly adorned with faint lightning, to enter
the silence of the Star Path. I give thanks for the Spirit of Approach-
ing Truth. Father, guide my actions. I shall light the Fire of Eternity
in continuance of the Dream. Will that flame be enough to fulfill
prophecy? These I meet in battle are darkened with ignorance.
Come, Kato'ya! I need to feel your blood within my veins!" When
he lifted his head, he saw the Aztecs headed toward him. The
leader had feathers dangling from his elaborate headdress. He
looked almost comically fierce with his painted face.

The leader made the others stop when he saw ancient Mokesh,
alone and standing his ground in defense of the canyon pass.
Because he was old, the leader taunted, "Aiyee! They have sent a
ghost to fight their battle! I am frightened." His body reflected
mock tremors of fear.

"Here, old woman! I have something to warm you up," the
Aztec leader said as he showed his teeth and fondled his genitals.

Mokesh felt his blood move faster in his heart as he spoke: "May
the Ancestors and Spirits bestow upon you health and peace. May
the Standing Tall People grow tall and green, and heal the illness
of your diseased. May All Our Relations return to the Circle of

Family in harmony. May Grandfather Sun bless you. May the blessings of this life and the next fall upon you. Return from whence you have come in friendship."

The Aztec leader laughed. "I will give you friendship, old man. I will plant my seed in your women, as I listen to the cries of your men as they seek the darkness of death."

Mokesh grew excited, but at the same time showed no emotion as he said: "Giver of All Life, guide me, and Ancient Ones, hear my voice. Banish these from the land."

The wind picked up and suddenly gusted around them, dust devils making it impossible to see.

The fight started. Mokesh told them of his medicine and spat his power in their direction. In this way, with the assistance of Old Man Thunder, he killed off the war party.

Many who heard the battle went to investigate after the silence had come. Many Aztecs had died, but the villagers were safe. They searched for Mokesh, but all that was discovered was a large golden-eyed rattlesnake basking in the glow of Grandfather Sun's light.

Tattooed Snake gashed his arms and legs with his knife. He cut his hair short and tore his white buckskin shirt. Thus he mourned for Mokesh. Tattooed Snake's daughter, Toho'ma, did indeed take Kokopelli as a mate and gave the gift of life to a son. Mokesh had done a great thing, and his fame endures.

The words presented here are not a fairy tale; they are a story.

Feeding the Flame

I awoke at dawn the morning of May 5, 2000, with an apprehensive joy in my heart. What would come to be known as the Grand

Alignment was upon humanity. An awakening of universal proportions was taking place, a time when the human community would embrace coming together in a circle, to share prayers and celebrate life. I sat up in bed and gave a shiver in the morning chill. The days had been hot but in the evenings we still required several blankets. I sat and listened to the steady *thunk! thunk! thunk!* of my heartbeat. It was the only sound.

I looked down at Lynda. Her loose dark hair fell about her face. I touched her soft skin. I was awed by the power of our love for one another. The quiet neighborhood seemed far away to me. But then the thought of the evening's gathering entered my mind and I arose.

I stood in the living room waiting for the coffee to brew. In the east the first streaks of orange crossed the sky. I smelled the grass, the sage with which I had purified, and smiled at our dog, who was watching me. I listened to the clear song of the kingbird crouched out back, trying to see in the kitchen window. Two crows flew through the sky toward where we would gather at sunset, their black bodies bobbing lightly through the morning sky. I looked around. It seemed like very little noise ever made it to our sanctuary.

As I watched the sky lighten, the whiffs of brewing coffee grew stronger. I stood in the quiet dawn, my heart beating with all the power of the Snake Clan. I felt ready for the Grand Alignment, and the energy this phenomenon had promised to bring.

I sat back on my haunches later that evening and looked down at the group of people gathering for the Grand Alignment. They were dancing around the sacred Eternal Flame. Of all the musical instruments created by humans since the beginning of time, the drum has been most widely used. It expresses the deep desire to make meaningful sounds. The beat of the surf, where the first air-breathing animals crawled out of Changing Mother's nursery to become land dwellers, is echoed in its cadence. It echoes the heartbeat of the first humans and still gives meanings to the rhythm of ceremonies and the pageantry of all cultures.

Memory stirred this night at the drum's cadence; the feet had become restless and the people who gathered had begun to align their body rhythms in the motion of the dance. It was a primordial urge, the echo of self-remembrance, the heartbeat, and the first ritual dance steps of humans in an attempt to celebrate life.

A voice led me back to the rock outcropping. I heard the drums and felt a breath on my neck. Coyote was behind me. The animal spoke. "The reality of imagination and dreams is life; being a part of humans, they will manifest." I looked into the Coyote's eyes and bit my lower lip.

I looked back toward the crowd below. They twisted and took on luminous forms until all were pure light. Humans, plants, mountains—all existed as living stars in the limitless space of my vision. Being endowed with motion, they danced and dazzled. Spirit's love manifested!

The Coyote rose and nosed something on the ground. A tooth lay at his feet. I lifted it to my heart. "Here is the offering of your family," he said. "Now all that exists is the power of love."

I looked at the tooth a second time. Coyote said, "For a while, Naylin 'iskiñihí, humanity was a shadow. The Dream makes the light, and you can see, touch, and hear All That Is. Through the Dream the reality of the time of peace will manifest. Laugh and celebrate life. Dreams have the power to heal and bring peace."

I watched Coyote cross the ridge. Near the top the animal turned and called, "The intangible becomes tangible in this time. Humanity stands in a position of actualization, able to reinforce the vision of the Fifth World of Peace and Illumination, able to reinforce the emancipating wisdom of All That Is and bring balance back to infinity; all they need do is ask for the guidance. We can help only when asked."

"Thank you, my uncle," I called. But Coyote had disappeared over the bluff.

As I turned to leave I saw in the glittering whiteness of the firelight below, the Children of the Universe dancing the patterns of the world before my eyes.

I awoke with a sudden jerk later that night. At first I didn't know where I was. I had been dreaming dreams that were contrary to the evening's events, that did not speak of peace, and that frightened me. I sat up quickly and felt a pain of anxiety in my chest. I struggled to breathe and was finally able to return to a relaxed pattern. I remembered Coyote and the message I had been given. The sun was not up yet, but I saw the morning star on the eastern horizon. I shook my head as though the whiteness of the stars had blinded me, or reminded me of another time and place.

When I awoke the second time, Nakía was kneeling beside me with Kato'ya and Coyote standing behind him. Nakía smiled at me, helped me up and held me tenderly to him as a brother might. He whispered in my ear, "The conflict of humanity is being exposed for healing. Remember the innocent in life, the delicate, the gossamer, the beautiful. A butterfly comes into the world with very little reason except to fly, mate, and make humanity's inner child smile. It does not question its destiny. It goes about its life happily." I felt his lips move against my hair, but was uncertain if I understood the words.

I touched Coyote as he came close. He looked anxiously into my eyes. "A butterfly is always attracted to the beautiful," said Coyote. "Whether it is the sun on a blade of grass or the edge of a deep ruby rose, the butterfly spends its brief time dwelling on loveliness."

"The anger and insanity will transform just as the butterfly sheds its cocoon," said Kato'ya. "The world is learning to honor the innocence in individual identity. Less time will be spent in dwelling on the ugly. Think of what is happening as the process of the butterfly. Honor it and embrace it as closely as possible in its gentle transition."

Nakía laughed and hugged me vigorously. As they faded into the darkness, I saw Lynda sleeping. I snuggled down next to her and returned to Dreamtime.

A Warrior of Light assesses the Shadow of Fear for the illusion contained within the shadow. He places himself strategically; no confrontation is ever a surprise. Integrity, generosity, and respect are his principles.

Love is the weapon. Therefore, a Warrior of Light heals all dysfunction contained within. He knows the Shadow of Fear has hundreds of tricks to lure a person into the confusion. He seeks to eliminate as many of his own issues as possible. In combat with the Shadow of Fear, he calls upon two aspects, wisdom and truth—these are his strategy and offense. Yet there will always be issues as long as there is evolution. Even for a Warrior of Light there will always be healing on new and unseen planes of existence. Only the Way of the Dreamer eliminates all dysfunction.

It is said that the Dreamer no longer has fear. This makes the Dreamer, who is one with all, a healed healer. The Warrior of Light accepts the battle with fear but does not see or go beyond it. The Dreamer goes beyond the concept of duality. The Dreamer knows that time is an illusion, that life is but one dream flowing into another, a fluctuating vibrational shift of life in continuum.

The Path of Beauty is a process of inner healing. The wounds of dysfunction can be the greatest weapons of the Shadow of Fear unless we find them all and heal them. This process takes time, but it is possible. If we remove these pitfalls of hurt and pain, we succeed in our healing and the Shadow of Fear has no chance to come back into our lives. How can we do this? We heal the source of what drew fear to us in the first place: the illusion of isolation and disconnection.

Salt River Prophecies

Some would say that "Salt River Prophecies" is the path I walk, the Good Red Road, the healing of the Universal Family. I was raised to believe that in order for us to be responsible co-creators of this world we need to ask ourselves if our actions hurt others. If they do not, then the need to express these ideas and inner desires should be exercised. Whatever you want to do, do it to the fullest. Life is our basic quest into our humanness. Fulfillment in life purpose is the eradication of all fears. This is spiritual realization.

The Legend

This is a true story, and it is legendary among the Snake Clan.

All over the canyon the small fires were being lit and the scent of wood smoke hung in the almost motionless air. Naylin Lagé estimated that there must be at least a hundred people spread out in the three-mile split in Changing Mother that sloped southward from the northern mouth. The northern space around the still unlit Central Fire had been left clear for the chajala, the Healing Dance of the Mountain Spirits. Once that was ablaze, too close would be too hot.

The canyon was an ideal place for a chajala, Naylin Lagé thought. The narrow canyon that opened up into this small meadow was almost perfect, and the short downland grass and lack of bushes or trees meant that there was nothing nearby that might catch fire. The trail into the canyon was so narrow that it was easily defended, yet it gave way to this beautiful secluded spot, giving appropriate dignity to this celebration beneath the holy summit home of the Mountain Spirits. The Tonto band of the Apache had been given this portion of the reservation to live on ten years earlier. Many worked at Camp Reno, gathering hay for the post contractor or serving as couriers and guides. Ever since this meadow had first been used secretly for the chajala (Naylin Lagé, now nineteen, had been brought to one of the earliest by her parents), sentries had been posted out of sight high above in the pass and along the trail. There were still some latecomers winding down the footpath in the twilight, spreading out to find space for their own temporary shelters and calling, *"Da-go-té!"* greetings to friends as they threaded their way among the already established family camps.

Each family circle was marked by a ring of white cornmeal laid on the grass.

Naylin Lagé and Massai were of the Chiricahua band and had traveled here with five others, six if you included four-year-old Ten Bears, who was bouncing excitedly at Naylin Lagé's side and announcing, "Da-go-té!" to everyone who passed, friend or stranger. Too bad that Massai's aunt, Red Horn, she of the large heart and the ironic tongue, could not be here tonight; but at eighty-two years old, climbing canyon trails, even for chajala, was no longer for her.

It was a close knit group, of which Naylin Lagé, as band healer, was proud. Massai had joked once that the group worked well because it contained the three phases of Changing Mother: the maiden soon to marry, Woodsong; Naylin Lagé, a mother; and shrewd Red Horn as the Yaya, or grandmother. Naylin Lagé knew that like so many of Massai's jokes, it was meant seriously.

"Which side does the pollen go, Mother?" Ten Bears asked, interrupting Naylin Lagé's thoughts. "I cannot properly remember."

"You should ask Woodsong, Little One. She is in charge of the altar tonight."

"Why, Mother? You are a healer, really."

"Because in a little while they will light that big fire in the middle, and everybody will go dance with the Mountain Spirits around it. Except for the very old ones, or those with little children, who will stay in their own spaces and watch. Your father and I will stay with you, but Woodsong and Two Strike will dance for us. So it's their special night, and they are Tlish Diyan. It is fair, is it not?"

"Why can I not dance too? Then we could all go?"

"Next year maybe. The dancing gets very fast, and you are a bit small for it yet."

"But I can run fast!"

"I know you can, Little One. But next year you will be a little taller and stronger."

"Like the Giver of All Life?"

"Not quite that tall," Naylin Lagé said with a laugh, looking toward the high canyon walls, where the very last rays of the setting sun reddened the crevices. It was unmistakably a gift of Creation. The Giver of All Life was the most gifted artist; the astonishing vitality of Changing Mother could shape the day if one but chose to look.

"I'm glad it is warm," Ten Bears said. "I don't like clothes."

"Me neither," Naylin Lagé agreed, enjoying the feel of the grass under her bare feet. Ten Bears was still young enough that clothes were an option, weather permitting; most children under the age of five were allowed the freedom of nudity during the warmer weather. Tonight the individual fires would help, of course, adding to the warmth of body and spirit. Naylin Lagé could remember the time she had run naked among the fires of her grandfather's camp. She was originally of the Warm Springs group of the Chiricahua. Her father, Santo, was the leader; and after the recent trouble following Cochise's death he had joined the Apache Scouts in an attempt to keep the peace that was such a fleeting commodity in their lives. This past year, peace had only been disturbed by a handful of incidents that, as the white agent had delightedly proclaimed, were instigated by a handful of renegade bands. And since the main war chiefs had settled their respective groups into the routine of reservation life, the repercussions were slight. There had been some arrests and a few deaths, and the land promised to the Apache still attracted its fair share of miners, about whom the Apache complained futilely.

Here and there in the canyon Naylin Lagé could make out different groups that were once sworn enemies, but in these days they would be as welcome as the rest. The tribe was too strongly rooted in band autonomy for anyone to impose superior rule.

Council meetings were composed of Chiefs and Holy Ones in various areas, and they provided what little organization was needed for the eleven Hedo-wa-chee. Each Summer Solstice the Clan Mothers would choose the leaders for war chiefs and peace chiefs. The appointed chiefs held their positions until the people no longer demonstrated confidence in their leadership abilities. Holy Ones needed no choosing; theirs was a lifetime apprenticeship to the miracles of life as dictated by Changing Mother and the Giver of All Life, and they were overseen by a teaching *'tsantí*.

The sun had set. It would not be long before the Mountain Spirit dancers and the Dreamer, Nochaydelklinne, made their ceremonial appearance.

Out of habit Naylin Lagé glanced around her own circle to make sure that all was in order, then reminded herself that tonight the responsibility was her apprentice's honor. North, east, south, and west stones had been placed. By the east stone a cloth had been laid upon the ground as an altar, with ritual representations of the Mountain Spirits and Kato'ya, the Snake Clan guardian and a distant mystical relative, arranged on the cloth. When the ritual part of the Chajala was over, the ceremonial objects would be packed away, the altar cloth folded, and the feasting would begin with the coming and going of friends.

A hush fell over the canyon and made Naylin Lagé look up. All eyes were turned to a small tent near the central fire and altar, the only enclosed structure in the whole canyon. Naylin Lagé's camp was about twenty feet from the tent, so she could clearly see the two men who had emerged and now stood flanking the doorway, in the light of the full deer moon, which was already bright. She knew them both: Nebigjay, one of Nochaydelklinne's brothers, and Nantiotish, another brother and a White Mountain war chief. Naylin Lagé felt a tremor of pride, for the Dreamer, in addition to being a noteworthy Coyotero Holy One, was also her favorite uncle.

Someone struck a single tone on a big drum and the assembly stood, facing the Central Fire and Altar. Ten Bears whimpered, wanting to see, and Massai lifted him to his shoulders.

The Dreamer appeared between the two warriors, and the watchers whispered their awed approval. He certainly looked like a fit representative of the prophecies: about fifty years of age, an honest, sober man. He was a 'tsantí of one of the largest bands and was known for his generosity and mildness. He was impartial in his dealings with those of all races and both genders. He moved with a calm dignity upon the breast of Changing Mother, while his brothers fell into step behind him. Then Delshay, leader of the Tonto, came into view. Again there was the brief whisper from the assembled Apaches, who were honoring this Chief of great standing.

The four made their way to the central fire and altar, where a huge fire was now blazing strongly enough to light up the canyon. Delshay picked up a torch, lit it from the fire, and presented it to Nebigjay. He held it aloft, pacing slowly to the many smaller unlit fire hearths that encircled the canyon, plunging into the kindling at the foot of each.

The Circle of Family blazed skyward, borne aloft by a roar of triumph from the throats of the Teñeh, the Children of the Wind. Naylin Lagé hugged Massai happily, and Ten Bears squealed anew, drumming his feet on his father's chest. Naylin Lagé rejoiced that the circle of fires was like it had been in the old days, marking, honoring, and reinforcing the cycle of the year. This was really something to be part of, this reborn hope for the future. No groveling self-abasement, no exploited hysteria—just this proud delight, this willing communion with the rhythms of nature, this joy before the Spirits of the Four Directions.

She suddenly realized that she had drifted off into formless thought, into an involuntary firelight gazing, when she felt Massai turning beside her. She pulled herself together, smiling; minutes must have passed. Nebigjay was already back at the central altar, silhouetted, and almost dwarfed against the great cliff sentinels of the canyon. Nochaydelklinne, smoldering pinyon in hand, was already on his way around the canyon, smudging and purifying the Circle of Family. This took time, for the canyon circle was a good half mile in diameter, but no one was impatient; everyone was mentally backing Nochaydelklinne, willing the "World of Peace, Love, Joy, and Truth" into being.

Down the slanting path, perhaps a mile away, a horse nickered briefly. Naylin Lagé felt a shared flicker of concern around her. But the feel of silence returned again, and the disturbance was forgotten.

Now Nochaydelklinne was once more before the altar, facing Nebigjay across it. His voice rang out in the night.

"Giver of All Life, your children stand before you. Ancestors, come again as of old onto our Sacred Mother. Lift up in the night to protect us. Put to flight the powers of evil. Give us days ending in peace and without suffering, a sense of unity with your natural world, and power through awareness of the world's patterns. Bring us to stand upon the Mountain of Vision and show us the World of Peace.

"I had a dream two sleeps ago," he said. He addressed them all but he looked at Naylin Lagé. "In this dream the Giver of All Life came down from the Sacred Lodge. He came on the Winds of Change. He was all dressed in fine buckskins and rode a fine painted horse. At first I was frightened, for I was sure he had come to deliver me to the Place of Souls. He laughed, and his laughter so filled me with wonder that I fell down to my knees. The Giver of All Life said, 'Rise. I have chosen you to deliver my message to the people. All the People of the Four Directions must dance together everywhere. They honor the Mother in celebration. A new time is coming where all will act as one. Kato'ya's return among those of the Star Nations will signal the beginning of this time. You must not hurt any living thing and you must walk your path in a good and right way always.'

"With that I found myself gazing on a wonderful scene, and from behind the crushing fear of the present I heard the songs of humanity. I heard the sound of bells announcing the beginning of prayer in the Kiva of Beauty. Bells molded in the ore of emotion and hung above the most sacred altar—the human heart.

"In the future I saw multitudes worshipping on the bosom of nature, their faces turned eastward and awaiting the inundation of Grandfather Sun's rays in the morning of truth. I saw the cities ruined, nothing remaining to tell of the ignorance that once prevailed. The Light of Truth shone brightly for all to see. I saw Elders seated under the shade of cottonwood trees, surrounded by the young, who were listening to tales of healing and renewal. I saw the young beating their drums and playing their flutes, and the maidens dancing under the oak trees. I saw people caring for the fields of plenty and singing songs of joy.

"I saw a woman dressed in flowers scented with impressions of the heart. I saw friendship strengthened between two-leggeds and All Our Relations. I saw the winged flying toward the brook. I saw the creepy crawly confident and secure.

"I saw no poverty, I saw no excess. I saw genuine love and equality prevailing among the Children of the Four Directions. I saw not one healer, for everyone had the power to heal themselves. I found no priest, for conscience had become the foundation of reverence. Treaties of amity and compassion were in force. I saw that the two-leggeds remembered they were part of Creation, and that they had raised themselves above the bitterness and separation, and had cast off the veil of confusion from the eyes of their collective soul. This soul once again could read what the clouds wrote on the face of the Infinite Void, and what the breeze drew on the surface of the water; this soul now understood the meaning of the flower's breath and the songs of the night birds.

"From this image of the future I saw Spirit and Beauty join in union with Life as their sacred ceremony. Spirit has shown me the promise of the Fifth World of Peace and Illumination. And I feel blessed."

He swept his hand in a clockwise direction, dropping sacred

power that popped and sizzled when it reached the fire. Nebigjay walked forward around the altar to join him. Delshay and Nantiotish stood next to them. Nantiotish held up his war lance, pointing downward and calling out in a voice resonant with authority, "Giver of All Life, look down with your eyes at your children. Let us see the truth. Giver of All Life, make us worthy of the gift of prophecy that you have brought to us this night. This is all I ask. It is enough!"

The silence was absolute as he thrust his staff into the fire. Nochaydelklinne, smiling, spread his arms wide and high summoning the Mountain Spirits, the Spirits of the Four Directions, and said, "Go forth and dance with the Spirits of the Four Directions, and become a spirit yourself. Bring back a gift of prophecy. Bring back the words of the Giver of All Life."

That was the signal. Before his voice had ceased, the Mountain Spirits had entered the circle and the tide was moving inward with them. Firelit bodies danced and called to the spirit of the land and the spirits of the Ancestors, weaving between the individual circles like river foam around rocks—inward, inward to the central Eternal Blaze, closing the circle as they reached it. Men danced in an outer circle with the women dancing in an inner circle, facing the men. Already the Circle Dance wheeled clockwise around the fire, with Nebigjay, Nantiotish, and Delshay falling in behind the Mountain Spirit dancers till the inward tide ceased flowing and all were in the ring, the head joining the tail. Nebigjay closed the circle. By the fire, Nochaydelklinne stood, still sprinkling sacred pollen on the passing dancers, blessing them.

Only a scattering of old people and baby-minders were left in the honeycomb of family circles, gazing inwards at the dancers, identifying with them. Naylin Lagé and Massai squatted with Ten Bears between them, their backs warmed by their own little fire, which Massai had just replenished.

"Who are those people?" Ten Bears asked.

"What people?" Naylin Lagé replied.

"Over there." The child pointed behind them, at the edge of the canyon, and they turned to look.

"Giver of All Life!" Massai said. "Trouble!"

There were perhaps thirty of them, Papagos, Pimas, Mexicans, and some Apaches, just appearing at the opening of the canyon pass, running in the shadows and heading toward the celebration. They must have crept through the pass unnoticed by the sentries on duty. But how? As Massai and Naylin Lagé watched, their number grew.

Naylin Lagé clenched her fists in a moment of blind fury then unclenched them, deliberately taking a deep breath. It was almost inevitable that someday the celebrations would be discovered. Perhaps it had been a bit arrogant to believe they could carry on the tradition without detection and uninterrupted.

Naylin Lagé frowned, puzzled. She did not understand. *Why could people not live together in peace and respect the beliefs of others? Why?* Naylin Lagé wondered.

The intruders, rifles aimed, were marching into the canyon, trampling straight through the little family circles toward the Great Fire, shouting, "Nochaydelklinne, come out! Show us your ghosts returned!"*

---

* I learned as a child that the Paiute prophet Wovoka participated in the Chajala and apprenticed to Nochaydelklinne. Nochaydelklinne was killed by U.S. troops before his movement reached much notoriety, and his teachings were kept alive in the isolation of the mountains of Mexico. Wovoka took what he learned and the visions he received to the other tribes, resulting in the well-known Ghost Dance. Wovoka's version of the Ghost Dance became a tornado that swept the land, yet by the time it reached the northern plains tribes—whose history with the movement is heart wrenching—much of what was passed was no longer recognizable as Wovoka's original intent.

Some of the older people not in the dance ran forward, trying to stop them. But the intruders were warriors, once dedicated to the same beliefs that were being practiced here tonight, and they easily swept the elderly bodies aside. The younger baby-minding fathers, like Massai, hesitated, torn between repelling the hostiles and standing guard over the children. Naylin Lagé grabbed at Massai arm, restraining him; he shrugged helplessly and acquiesced.

The dancers had heard the chanting and had turned, incredulous anger in their faces. The intruders did not pause, instead heading straight for Nochaydelklinne, who was clearly their target.

The shouting changed to the voice of one man, Sergeant Mose. "Enjuh, it is well!" he exclaimed. "I come to kill my brother!"

That was all it took to break the Circle. The dancers swept down on the invaders, weapons or no weapons. The group swayed and fell in a mass of bodies.

Ten Bears was sobbing now. Naylin Lagé, hugging him fiercely, cried out, "Massai! Look! Uncle's tent!"

As she pointed, the tent of the Dreamer tottered and fell. More intruders, unnoticed until now, were tearing the canvas into great strips and scattering them about the grounds.

Naylin Lagé screamed an astonished "No!"

It was then that the unbelievable happened. The ground beneath them, the whole of the canyon, moved, throwing attackers and defenders alike off their feet. It lasted for only a few seconds, but in those seconds the canyon groaned like a giant in pain. Then it was still.

After the turmoil there was a moment of silence—the silence of complete shock.

Nochaydelklinne was first on his feet. "Come to us! Show yourselves to us again," he called to the spirits. "Tell us, your people, what we must do."

Sergeant Mose sprang up and dragged down Nochaydelklinne,

and the fight was on again. Above the screaming and the shouting and the tears came the sound of hooves, pounding up the long slanting pathway.

Naylin Lagé and Massai stood stunned, no longer able to take it all in. Even Ten Bears, clutched between them, was soundless and trembling. The Sixth Cavalry, a dozen horsemen, charged into the canyon, sweeping into the circle around the melee, herding it toward the fire like sheep. Massai shook Naylin Lagé out of her paralysis, shouting to her over the din, "Run! Quick!"

Suddenly and desperately active, Naylin Lagé swept the little altar bare and tore open her bag, flinging the sacred items into it. Woodsong and Two Strike ran up and joined them. How they had dodged through the cordon of horses Naylin Lagé had no time to wonder.

While grabbing Ten Bears she heard Two Strike shout to Massai, "Got to get the women out of this!" Massai nodded grimly.

Two Strike grabbed his weapons, with Massai waving him to go on. By instinct the four of them grabbed their weapons, sticking knives into their belts, and taking rifles in hand. Then they ran. Massai held Ten Bears in his arms.

The cavalry was tightening and loosening their ring, teasing the crowd inside it. Two Strike, in the lead, saw that toward the central fire was the clearest path and he headed for it. But as he reached it he halted in his tracks, staring down.

Naylin Lagé followed his look, and screamed again the one word "NO!"

Dead, a military bayonet impaled through his belly and staring upward, lay Delshay—the brave Delshay, their friend.

Massai pulled Naylin Lagé away roughly. Through her tears she saw Nantiotish, berserk in his anger, a burning log in his hand, leap crazily between two horsemen and run to the dead chief of the

Tonto. Standing over him, he flung the log at a passing horse. The rider burst into flame, colliding with the next in line, who swerved aside and then fell. The hemmed-in crowd saw Nantiotish and copied his actions. All at once the hunters became the hunted, trying to escape a shower of blazing bullets.

Massai almost swept Naylin Lagé off her feet, hustling her over the edge of a cliff path, away from the horror.

There was one more earth tremor as the five of them stumbled up the path toward White River. But it was slight, and stunned by all that had happened, they barely noticed it. A strange sound rose from the canyon, a weird half-wail, half-exultation, the frenzy of despair and revenge. It was the death chant.

Nochaydelklinne had escaped, and he and his following would return again and again to Carrizo Creek in the Cibeque area and continue dancing. In August 1881 he would pass his power to his niece, Naylin Lagé. Members of the Apache Scouts later assassinated Nochaydelklinne, and the final days for his followers were tragic; the last gathering was subdued in a bloody battle in November 1881. Naylin Lagé and her family would seek sanctuary in the mountain stronghold of Old Mexico, where the prophecies would be held and nurtured in secrecy.

Gate of Rebirth

The sun was at its midpoint, almost directly overhead. The nights had become warmer and the days longer. I liked this season, for it promised nothing. The summer was nearly upon us, we had our own place, and we could take time for ourselves and just be. I would soon journey to cry for a vision. I wanted to sit in silence with my ancestors and bask in the full moon's glow. I was thankful to be here in this time and place.

"Wake up, Naylin 'iskiñihí!" I was hit on the shoulder. "Naylin 'iskiñihí!"

I rolled onto my back and rubbed my eyes. My head hurt.

"Naylin 'iskiñihí! Naylin 'iskiñihí!"

I opened my eyes and looked at Nakía. With great effort I propped myself up on an elbow and rubbed my head. I had run into the wall in the dark on my way to the bathroom that night and now had a headache. I sat up. Nakía had been around a lot since the Passing of Power Ritual, where the spirit of my grandfather passed the title and power of the 'tsantí, the Web Dreamer, to me.

"Yes! Naylin 'iskiñihí, your stories are not just stories," Nakía said. "They are also an expression of energy."

"Energy?"

"The source of the energy is physical, rooted in the genetic chemistry of your body. Self-realization refines this energy for spiritual power. Self-actualization, for you, is therefore a psycho-physical process; it is a state of being rather than a mere intellectual understanding of your process."

Nakía—the snake son of our clan guardian, Kato'ya—stood before me grinning like an idiot. Kato'ya was in the process of passing his power to Nakía much in the same manner that Grandfather had passed his to me. But how was that happening? The stories and prophecies had triggered something within me, a healing of extraordinary magnitude. I was changing, learning the full meaning of what a 'tsantí actually was. Grandfather would have said it was my many selves learning to coexist in the many magical worlds available for my true nature to access. This process produced prophetic teaching dreams with strong meaning and symbolism that were driving me bonkers.

Vision Quest would provide me with the opportunity to unlock old patterns, meet death as my friend, and change, transform, and transmute. The transformation that had begun with the Passage of Power was a process of realizing my destiny. I would learn to fly with Tocha, the hummingbird, if I was capable of flowing in resonance with the natural processes of change.

Nakía was talking about energy. "The energy has been awakened, and you must draw it upward. The force begins at your genitals and rises up your spine. On its way it nourishes your kidneys, nerves, and blood vessels. When it passes the base of your skull the nervous system and lower parts of the brain are being stimulated. This is the source of your anxiety and emotional roller coaster."

"The source of my anger?"

"Yes. Reaching the crown, the river of energy is opening your entire subconscious potential as a 'tsantí and human. Descending downward, it nourishes your eyes, your senses, your vital organs." Nakía stood and walked to the other side of the room. He bent down and pointed at Little Wolf, using her as a sort of teacher's model, following snake lines along her body with his finger. "Cascading toward your navel, it returns to the loins again, ready to be drawn into another circuit. From your studies you know that to work magic in the Fifth World paradigm it is necessary to reprogram the first eight circuits now. Just as all existence operates on a continuum between the physical and the most subtle, so too do you need to utilize all parts of your body, mind, and spirit for success."

I smiled and forgot about my aching head for a moment.

"The story you work on now, it belongs to your great-grandmother and your grandfather. It was given to you with loving heart. Yes, the story of 'The Salt River Prophecies.' You must release your anger to tell it."

Nakía walked back to the bed. He touched my head.

"Why is there such turmoil within me?" I queried.

"You are embarking into the unknown. You cannot see or anticipate where Spirit will lead you. Trust with certainty that you will be safely led through the Shadow of Fear. You are learning a new dimension of trust, and your body is evolving with this leap of faith. You are fulfilling the purpose for which you were created."

I looked at Nakía and my heart jumped. Nakía hugged me.

I worked most of that afternoon. It was quiet. I stood up and flexed my legs. My body was sore from the stillness. I breathed deeply and looked around the house. It was good for Lynda and me to finally have our own space. I was glad that Vision Quest was only a day away; it would be a chance to clean my mind and renew my spirit. The last time I had been on the hill was nearly ten years before. I had been shown then that my great-grandmother, Naylin Lagé, and I were of one spirit—evolution unfolding.

In the morning we would journey for my quest. This night I would make the offering of prayer ties to the sacred Changing Mother, so that blessings might fall on me, my family, and the land. The sacred Stone People Lodge had been prepared. Soon the Eternal Flame would be lit. It would blaze high, then it would be allowed to burn down so that the record keepers of time, the Stone People, glowing red hot, could be gathered and transported into the lodge. We would purify with sage, sing songs of victories and honoring, and pray that our requests for guidance would be heard. The thought of the steam rolling off the inside walls of the lodge, cascading down our bodies, and joining with our sweat made me wish time would travel faster so that I could be enclosed there in the Sacred Womb of Dreamtime. The Stone People would provide images for us to look down upon, and the Giver of All Life would send messengers to show us the way.

I went into the bedroom and sat on the bed. I stretched out my legs, leaned back, and closed my eyes. I knew I had work to do, but the emotional roller coaster I had been riding was tiring and I needed the rest.

I awoke to the sound of laughter. I sat up quickly and bumped my head on the wall. "Oh," I said, "ouch!" Banging my head twice in a twenty-four-hour period was a definite sign that I was in need of grounding. The laughter grew louder. To my right I could see the sun starting to set. It was late in the afternoon. I scrambled to my feet and went to the living room. "Who is it?" I said. "Who laughs at me when I hurt this way?" I spun around.

"Easy, Little One," croaked Nakía. "Why are you being so hard on yourself?" I looked down. He continued, "All life pulses. Information is being received. You are going from a nine-wave cycle of chaos to the thirteen-wave cycle of harmony. Do you believe the currents of the dragon will not affect you? You have been led to this phase of your existence so that you will depend and preserve your sacredness and that of the Tlish Diyan. You must harmonize and distribute the energy of Changing Mother in accordance with daily life."

I heard the words. I turned to Nakía and said, "I have been working on the story and I feel much better. Just tired."

"You have been given the gift of purpose. The fact that you are still alive after a lifetime of death and near-death experiences validates that fact. Your pleasure with that purpose is best expressed by the fullness with which you greet and live the traditions you have been given." Nakía smiled. "Do not run from the invitation your experiences now offer. It gives you a chance, a bit different from the chances you have had before, to fulfill part of your purpose in the evolutionary process of yourself and others."

"I have stalked power and knowledge all day in working with this legend," I said. "I thought to lay down my head, that rest would help me assimilate what has been presented."

"It has been said that the most prayerful life is the one most actively lived. A full encounter with each moment is evidence of your trust in the Now and thus our trust in your higher power. You are very diligent in these things. Healing is helping you remember, releasing you to participate more actively in the special circumstances of your life."

"You speak the truth," I admitted. "When I look around, I know that the people who seek me out need my best efforts. They're not here by accident but by Spirit's design."

"Offer them the best you have," Nakía said as he sat on the couch. He scratched his back. The he cocked his head and looked across the living room at me. "Acceptance, love, support, your prayers—know that it is Spirit's plan for your life and theirs."

I was surprised to see that Nakía's faintly visible whiskers were white, like those of an old coyote. But his eyes were still the palest blue.

Nakía laughed softly. "Look into my eyes. See the great power. See the truth of prophecy."

The Tlish Diyan believe that we manifest the future through our visions, dreams, thoughts, and actions. We are co-creators of the world we live in. By taking responsibility and integrity to heart in understanding this phenomenon, by projecting pure intent and receiving its echoes, the World of Peace, Love, Joy, and Truth becomes reality. It is only through responsible co-creation of our reality that we achieve full potential.

Looking down the hallways of time, there are many terrible things that have transpired during the Fourth World of Separation. They are there, a part of history, a part of our lives. But in healing and moving forward comes the ease of understanding. The security that we long for and discover has been ours all along. All we needed to do was move forward with trust.

As we stand before the unknown, the Shadow of Fear may attempt to overwhelm us. But the choice available to us now and always is to see through the illusion of our aloneness. Spirit shares the space we're in at all times, and when combined our abilities can manifest responsibly the very best for all.

Our lives are being eased in direct proportion to our faith in our connection to Spirit, our every concern is being cared for, and experiences we need to grow from are being placed before us. We can let go of our anguish, our doubts, and our fears. Infinite peace is ours for the seeing.

Kato'ya's Return

Throughout the production of this work my partnership with Spirit—walking the Blue Road—compelled me to ask myself what attributes I was demonstrating that would draw many of these lessons to me. The wonderful part of this partnership was that all the resources for answering my questions were within me. Many times I found I needed to reach deep within and use the utmost of my abilities to manifest my dream. This is a continuing effort in my personal evolution.

It has taken many years for the Blue Road of Spirit to meet the Good Red Road I have been destined to walk. "Kato'ya's Return" brought my sacred purpose out of the future and into Now. I express my thanks to my clan guardian. I am happy for what I have been given, and that I have a community with which I am able to share. My appreciation for my life is born of my gratitude for the beauty of the world.

The Prophecies

As I contemplated "Kato'ya's Return," I became dimly aware of a swift, bright buzzing sound near me. The sound moved farther away. As it darted close, I saw a ruby-throated hummingbird hovering curiously in the air in front of me. The light of the late afternoon shone so strongly through the bird's delicate feathers that it seemed transparent, like a tiny rainbow.

I had to smile as the tiny winged one swung gently back and forth, oscillating in the air. Its humming enveloped me in a delicate bubble of sound and I could almost feel the air driven by its swift wings. All the while it studied me curiously with its black eyes.

I gazed into the darkness there, aware of my Siberian husky gliding soundlessly through the shadows.

With a sigh, I closed my eyes and beheld a vision of the most beautiful vivid rainbow I have ever seen. The arc of shimmering luminous colors remained ever present as I moved through it. The mist of red light surrounded me and my physical body became completely relaxed. Then the red dissolved into orange and I became healed. The orange blended into yellow and I was immersed in the sensation of devoted love. I witnessed all those who shared my life as happy and whole. The yellow became green, the green of grass and the leaves—the nurturing force of the Sacred Parents' power—and that vital force rippled through my being. The green softened into blue and my balanced ego ran to embrace my inner child, and together we witnessed the manifestation of humanity's dreams. The blue then blended into indigo and higher self joined balanced ego and inner child, the completion of my trinity within. The indigo then faded to violet and the power of All That Is bore me up into the vast Medicine Bowl of Eternity. I felt light and calm and filled with radiant light.

I became aware of my breathing as the dog rubbed against my leg. Opening my eyes, I felt peaceful yet very much alive. A tremor of excitement moved excruciatingly slowly down my body, radiating to all parts of me, then moving straight to my heart where it lingered and ignited a soft, sweet fire——a sensation I have known many times before, one that takes root deep inside me and blossoms like a summer rose.

There are many colors in the rainbow, and most of us have heard the prophecy, in one form or another, of the Rainbow Warriors and the Fifth World of Peace and Illumination. Through this prophecy we have been taught that with spiritual support the Rainbow Warriors—people of all colors and faiths—will join together, eventually establishing a long and joyous reign of peace.

Many indigenous traditions have held similar versions of this prophecy. From the Return of White Buffalo Calf Woman in the form of Miracle, the white buffalo calf born in 1994, to the Return of Kato'ya in March 1998, signs or omens that foretell the fulfillment of this prophecy are becoming an everyday occurrence around the world.

The Tlish Diyan legend of "Kato'ya's Return" sharply mirrors the Toltec legend of Quetzalcoatl, that of the Mayan Kukulkan, and Con-tici of the Inca. This entity of light, by whatever name you use, was a teacher of love whose lessons to humanity spoke of spiritual strength, connection, honor, mercy, and kindness. The teachings embody the love and unity of people who merge their hearts and work to fulfill the prophecies of peace and harmony.

As was foretold by Nochaydelklinne and the historical legends of the Tlish Diyan, Kato'ya's Return has indeed come to pass. On March 21, 1998, a celestial sign marked the moment of activation between Earth and human consciousness. A cosmic snake constructed from the alignment of Mercury, Saturn, and Mars to form the head was followed by the sun, Jupiter, Venus, Neptune, the moon, and Pluto at the root of the tail. The cosmic serpent was headed toward the Pleiades, marking this cycle of time as an awakening of inner connection to the unconditional love of the Universe. As these planets moved across the heavens many began to tune into planetary interconnection and an understanding of humanity's intimate connection with our own inner wisdom.

According to the legends of the Apache Tlish Diyan this began what is known as the Thirteen Sacred Mirrors of Fire. This is a process aided by forces throughout the universe in which healing, recognition, and self-actualization occur; this is what New Age people have referred to as Ascension.

Each of the Thirteen Sacred Mirrors of Fire is an awakening of spiritual and genetic records that we carry within us concerning our evolution. This period contains thirteen cycles of purification, learning, and preparation, with each lasting the equivalent of one solar year. It correlates with the popular concept that 2012 is the projected year of enlightenment.

The entire path is a journey of exploration, discovering the truth of where experience lies. We are opening ourselves to what is unique and throwing off the illusion of limitation, and evolving an outer resonance connected to the mysteries of the universe.

The Thirteen Sacred Mirrors of Fire are situations created to assist us in knowing ourselves as complete and healed spiritual individuals. The process is a quest that delivers us into the wonders of the Fifth World of Peace and Illumination.

I am honored to be able to share with you a few of the keys to unraveling the mysteries contained within the Thirteen Sacred Mirrors of Fire that my grandfather provided more than thirty years ago. Keep in mind that each Sacred Mirror cycle is approximately one year.

First Sacred Mirror of Fire

> *Thunder and rain at night. Growth comes with a shock.*
> *Expression and duration appear in the first moment.*
> *Things snap into focus. Pursue unity in life. Monstrous*
> *vision in fragments; haunt. Gathered glimpses and*
> *inferences bring sense. Mysterious life comes together.*
> *Thirteen Sacred Mirrors reveal the whole.*
> *Go the distance . . .*

When the First Sacred Mirror of Fire was ushered in at the time of the Spring Equinox in 1998, Humanity really began to learn that things could not remain the same forever. We may have felt that this insight came suddenly, and yet, in actuality, this time has emerged as the product of unseen cycles.

When we entered this physical plane we carried with us the complete pattern for our evolution and that of our planet. This transition completely embodies our destiny.

The First Sacred Mirror showed us that as long as we continued to grow in our spiritual connection, welcomed All Our Relations as family, and continually sought to expand our understanding of ourselves and the world around us, we were engaging in the ultimate creation of self and future.

As we entered this new phase of existence, it became necessary to re-examine our changing parameters, revamping ourselves according to individual situations. The task that came to pass was a challenge to remove labels, both inside and out. This included the realization that we are co-creators of our world.

To continue our growth we were challenged. The compassion of humanity was exercised. The challenges, many times, were difficult, but in the end we were gifted with outcomes that excited us and helped our spirits to soar. Slowly destiny began to be revealed.

We would still have to make changes and adjustments as our true purpose is clarified. What resulted within this time frame was a sense of needing to return home and connect, and a tremendous feeling of assurance that we could accomplish this task.

Second Sacred Mirror of Fire

> *In one arbitrary stroke, Life is suddenly decided. Worship*
> *with conscience, and receive grace with humility. Guide*
> *with awareness. Lead with modesty.*

The Second Sacred Mirror of Fire led us to issues contained within ancestral family dynamics. We began to examine the validity of concepts we were taught as children. The facts were presented for consideration.

Everyone has been compelled to examine the ongoing circumstances in our lives and what part early relationships played in our ability to make decisions clearly and wisely in the present. We discovered that many of us no longer wished to play out a karmic interlude of victimization. We made a conscious decision to embrace forgiveness, gratitude, and appreciation. Humanity began to focus its self-awareness. We have moved into acting with a conscience, seeking leadership that walks its talk without hidden agendas or the manipulation and abuse of power. We are stepping into maturity as Children of the Universe and we welcome the insight that we need to be responsible for all our actions.

Third Sacred Mirror of Fire

> *No audience is needed to open the heart. Scale the seven*
> *stars of the dipper, hollow the space between Sky and*
> *Earth. Transcend the limitations of time.*

With the coming of the Third Sacred Mirror of Fire, situations are created that demonstrate that our connection to nature has value because it is built on a qualitative foundation. The ancient sages became venerable through acquired knowledge, a healthy dose of experience, experimentation, and contemplation. Theories and practices such as Einstein's theory of relativity, the superstrings theory, and applied ecopsychology have only begun to grasp at the full understanding of the internal workings of the universe. During this Sacred Mirror we intuit special connections between facts that open many new avenues of understanding.

This Sacred Mirror is a time of evolving lifestyle. We have perspective and vigor, and we are receptive to learning from one another in ways shaped by our choices, thus transcending the previously self-imposed limitations. We express our personal truth and begin to define the future.

Fourth Sacred Mirror of Fire

> *All life is one whole. Powerful sound. Potential silence.*
> *Confusion removed with kaleidoscopic reality. Wisdom*
> *and courage bring responsible action.*

The Fourth Sacred Mirror of Fire is the point where the quiescence of spiritual devotion and the activeness of living integrate. Anxiety melts away from human consciousness as we live spiritual lives and realize that we are all part of the same seamless whole.

By this stage of our healing we realize that there is no prospect of stopping the process. The mere act of proceeding brings its own reward: transformation. A feeling of overwhelming serenity silences the committee within.

The vortex of energy at this time contains the understanding of all to come. Action is guided by both intellect and experience. It is a time when we test ourselves in the knowledge we have acquired. With wisdom, courage, timing, and perseverance our evolutionary progression is sound. Kato'ya passes his power to Nakía, the new Snake Clan guardian of the Fifth World. The cycle is complete, and transition is at hand.

I have shared here interpretations of the first wheel, the Vibral Core. I would like to give each of you the opportunity to stretch your own intuitive powers by providing you with just the clues for the remaining Mirrors. Remember that free will is ever-changing and ever-evolving; interpretations of the Mirrors that may seem correct from today's perspective may be dynamically altered according to the world perspective tomorrow. This is the magic and knowledge contained within the universe. Truth is what rings true deep within your being.

Fifth Sacred Mirror of Fire

Mountain Spirits divulge their secrets. Strength brings discovery. Wind from the cave, movement in the stillness. Power found in silence. Shimmering horizon, settling of the sky. See sound. Hear light. United senses. Expressed meaning . . .

Sixth Sacred Mirror of Fire

Classical and absurd are no longer seen. Shared knowledge lives as many are fed. Songs of the Fourth World of Separation fade into the landscape of time . . .

Seventh Sacred Mirror of Fire

Earth Mother's fissures soften, desiccation dissolves. Balance comes once again. Methods change quickly . . .

Eighth Sacred Mirror of Fire

*Shared experience is given. Completion brings fulfillment.
Fulfillment brings liberation. Liberation brings life's
infinite continuance. A test has been passed. Soaring
with Hawk becomes natural. Untangling the web of
concordances, the world is better. Trust in Spirit within.
Acceptance is given. Illusion is no longer reality's border.
Pierce fear to go beyond . . .*

Ninth Sacred Mirror of Fire

*Mute black night. Crimson light through pine shadows,
as the fire sun brings Moon of Four Eclipses.
Pure light in all colors . . .*

Tenth Sacred Mirror of Fire

*True links do respond. Reunion of Family, after many
years forced apart. Love proves true as ever. Storm breaks
into pieces, clouds charge the horizon. Revolving of
heavens generates the start. Nurturing quality of freedom.
Imagination-built bridge, no more deceiving . . .*

Eleventh Sacred Mirror of Fire

*Cooperation. Perception, experience, connection shows
when to lead and when to follow. Hummingbird
iridescence in vertical shadows, violet blooms spread to
noonday sun.
The world's beauty a swirl of color, in the
heart's center the bright still Creator.
Receiving without complaint, basking in new fate . . .*

Twelfth Sacred Mirror of Fire

> *Communication through image. Infinite*
> *sacred points of view. Drinking water*
> *carries us to the Source . . .*

Thirteenth Sacred Mirror of Fire

> *Human nature is one, we are whole. Desire and pursuit*
> *of the whole is unconditional love. Spokes on the*
> *Wheel of Life keep evolution constant . . .*

The Tlish Diyan place great value on these ancient prophecies. The Thirteen Sacred Mirrors of Fire are like a river with a long course, a living and valid aid in our evolution. They bring freshness, richness, and fertility.

What makes the prophecies of the traditional indigenous people so relevant today? The adherents are fully manifesting the greatness of their insight in the now, today. To move with the flow of the prophecies into this new and enlightening age of human consciousness is to heal and change.

We are seeking to heal and change by being one with the Earth Mother. She is a magician that decided to become who she is millions of snows ago, just so life as we know it could be born.

E-chi-ca-say, All Our Relations, to Earth we are each precious, wondrous. When we will ourselves to change we too are creating magic. Think of this new millennium as the most beautiful bowl you can imagine. We possess this bowl; it is our present and future. We can carve it anyway we wish. We are creating beauty and manifesting the power of Spirit.

These are the dynamics of manifesting vision and fulfilling prophecy. Think about it. We are launching rafts onto the great river of our own creativity so that we may see the gifts we already carry within.

What can we say to people if it is not the silent word of our own example and caring? Each act of love kindles self-love in another. The beauty we touch here is a trail that we walk together. Spirit is struggling through a blessed journey of transformation into a new world of light. The mother and her children are of one mind.

Daaiina, and so it is . . .

Epilogue

Do you know what it's like to write a book? I started out saying it would be easy; Grandfather had given me the stories, and all I needed to do was write them down in a way that would have the power to express something vital—something unforgettable—about the individuals, places, or events. The challenge was to transcend cultural differences and touch an understanding within the heart that rose above those differences.

I have proposed a worldview that has been embraced, until recently, largely by indigenous peoples of the world and in secrecy. The words and symbolism were designed to paint images that will bestow an insight into a unique perspective.

In this kaleidoscopic range of stories, I found a medicine wheel of Healing that would forever change my life and usher in the next phase of my evolutionary process. I would like to share but a few rare insights that were offered to complex questions I came across during the birthing of this work.

Everyone has his or her own way in life. We can learn from each other, although we can never have what the other possesses. We are each shaped by our experiences, and to transcend our limitations through healing is truly our combined destiny.

I welcome those who have journeyed through time with me. I invite you to recognize your connection to All That Is. Please write to me and tell me your opinions and your hopes. But be advised: My solemn hope for the future is to go on titillating your aural senses with the echoes of the ancient storytelling tradition.

Hiyaa gozhoo dolee, "May peace and love flow."

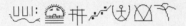

Maria Yracébûrû
E-mail: earthwisdom@earthlink.net
Web site: http://home.earthlink.net/~earthwisdom

Books of Related Interest

WALKING ON THE WIND
Cherokee Teachings for Harmony and Balance
by Michael Garrett

MEDITATIONS WITH THE CHEROKEE
Prayers, Songs, and Stories of Healing and Harmony
by J. T. Garrett

MEDITATIONS WITH THE NAVAJO
Prayers, Songs, and Stories of Healing and Harmony
by Gerald Hausman

MEDITATIONS WITH THE HOPI
by Robert Boissiere

NAVAHO SYMBOLS OF HEALING
A Jungian Exploration of Ritual, Image, and Medicine
by Donald Sandner, M.D.

THE WORLD IS AS YOU DREAM IT
Shamanic Teachings from the Amazon and Andes
by John Perkins

ORIGINAL WISDOM
Stories of an Ancient Way of Knowing
by Robert Wolff

THE TOLTEC PATH OF RECAPITULATION
Healing Your Past to Free Your Soul
by Victor Sanchez

DANCE OF THE FOUR WINDS
Secrets of the Inca Medicine Wheel
by Alberto Villoldo and Erik Jendresen

Inner Traditions • Bear & Company
P.O. Box 388
Rochester, VT 05767
1-800-246-8648
www.InnerTraditions.com

Or contact your local bookseller